BLOW-UPS

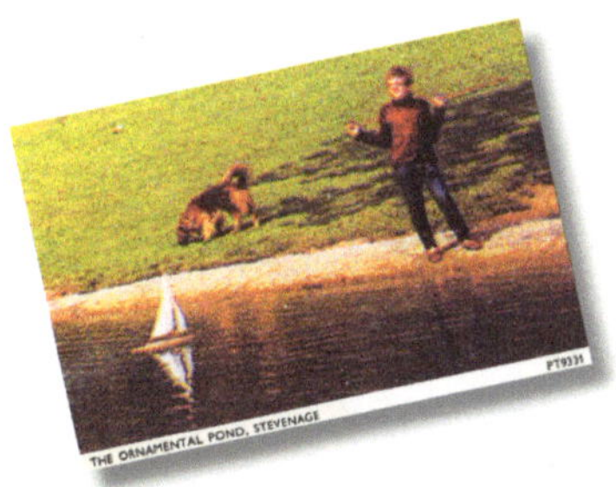

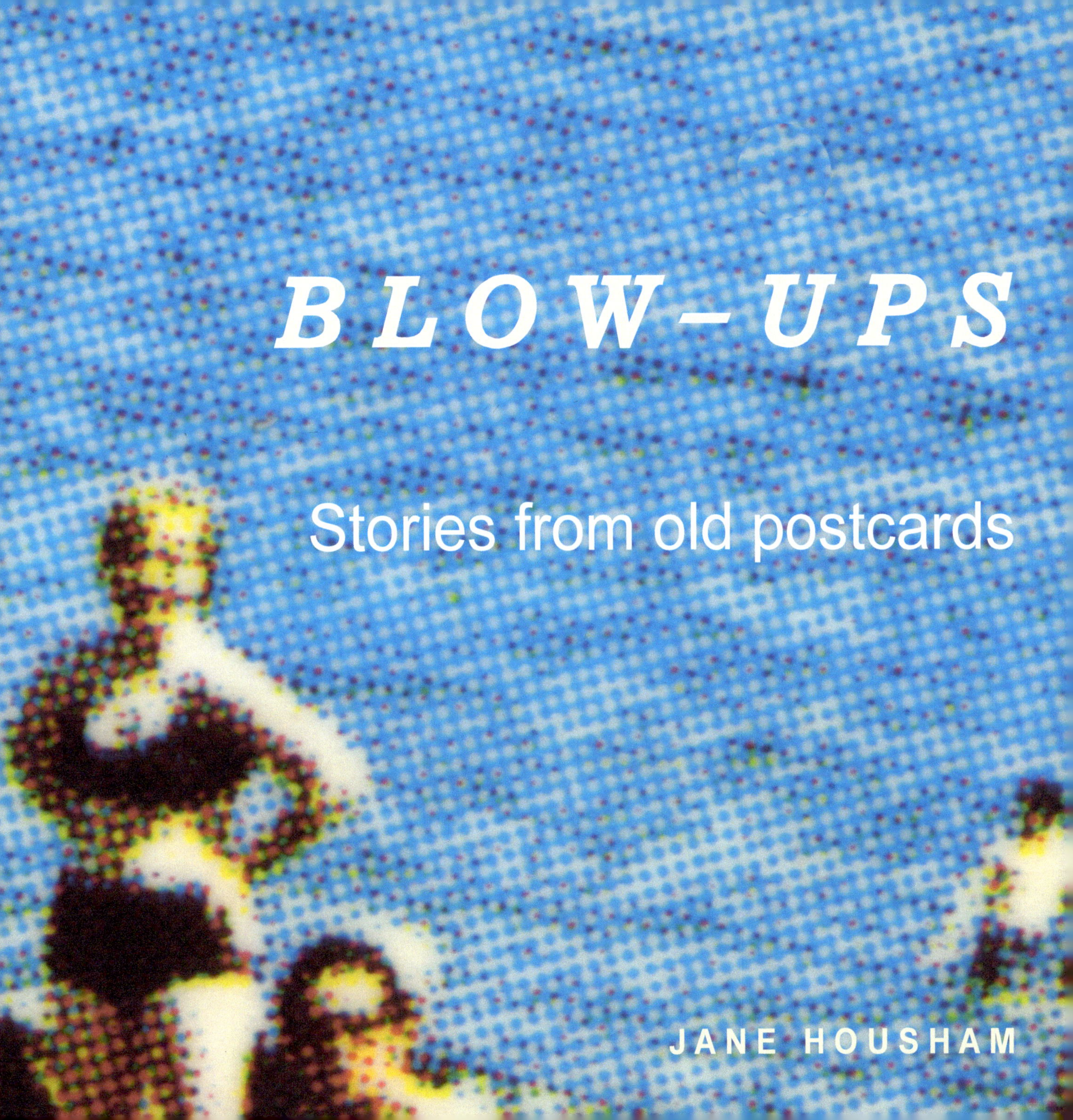

BLOW-UPS
Stories from old postcards
JANE HOUSHAM

First published in 2021 by Jane Housham
11 Offley Road, Hitchin SG5 2AZ, UK

Copyright © Jane Housham 2021
The moral right of the author has been asserted. All rights reserved.

ISBN 978-1-9196197-0-5

The author is grateful for the kind permission of John Hinde Ltd
to reproduce the images on the cover and on pages 14, 15,
30, 32, 33, 45, 47 and 63.
And for the kind permission of Elgate Products Ltd
to reproduce the images on pages 12 and 13.

Every effort has been made to secure the appropriate permissions to
reproduce images in this book. If there has been any oversight,
I will be happy to rectify the situation as soon as possible.

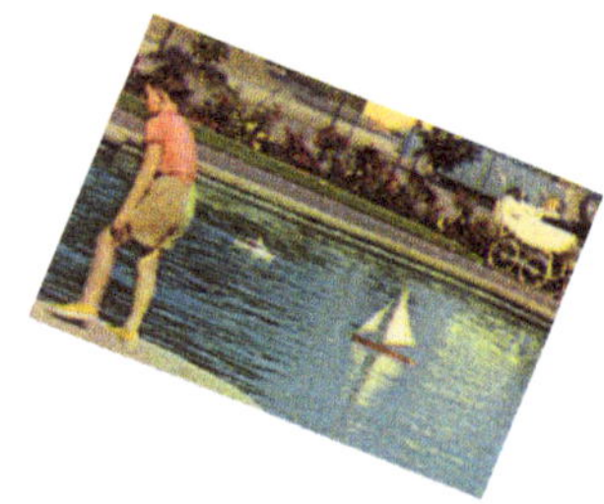

THE STORIES

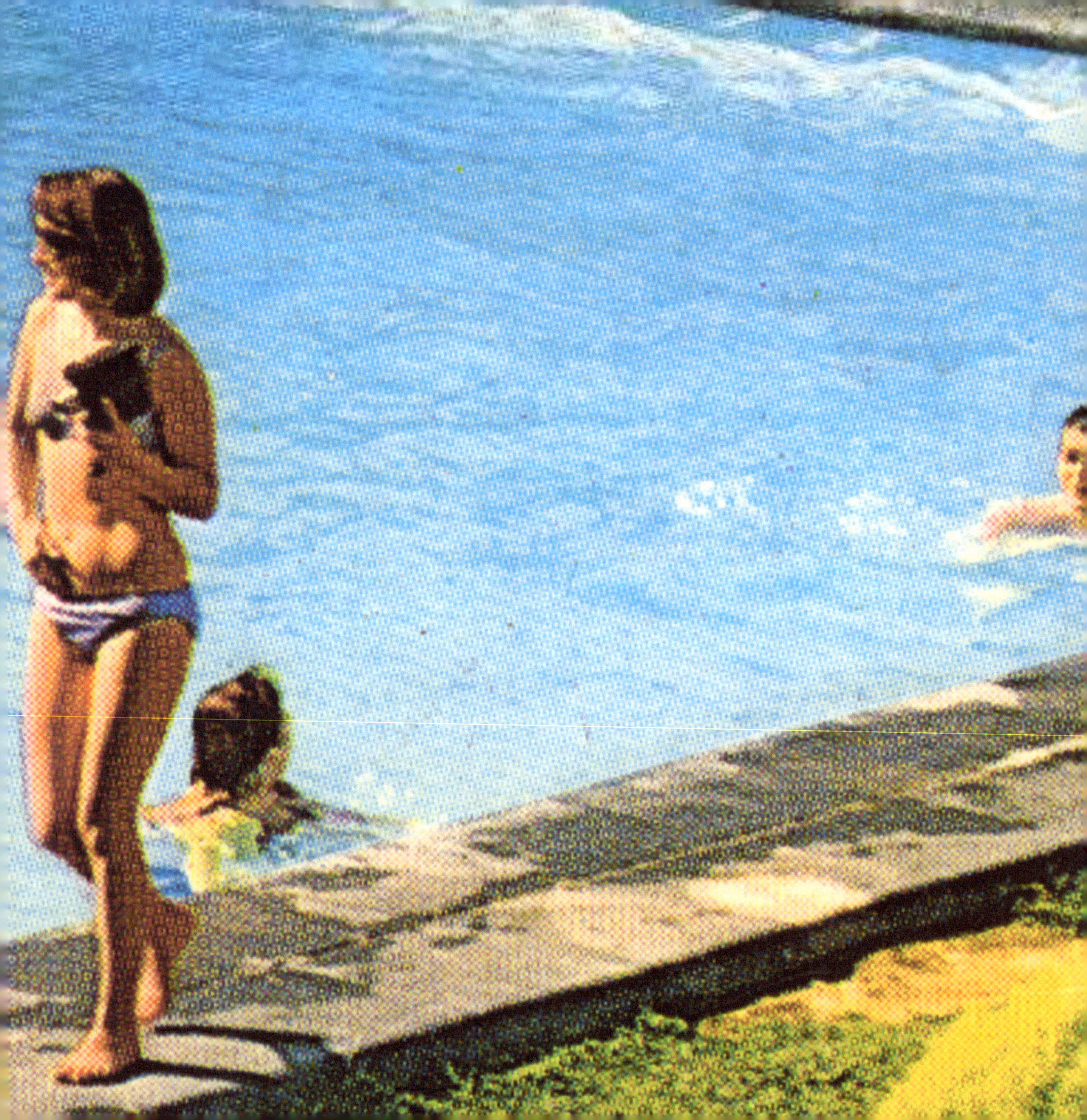

INTRODUCTION

Picture postcards from the past are a wonderful resource. Used to send brief and often inconsequential communiques in the heyday of the postal system, they were the text messages of their day, benefitting from multiple daily collections and deliveries. To begin with, from 1870, only the Post Office printed postcards and they had no pictures on them. Then, in 1894 – happy day! – the Post Office permitted other firms to print postcards and these could also have a picture on the front. Picture-postcard collecting became a craze in Europe and the United States, particularly amongst women, and cards winged their way around the globe with abandon. You were only supposed to write the address on the back as it was felt to be unseemly to send a message that could be seen by all and sundry. However, the urge to send love and kisses and all manner of other things was too strong to be

suppressed and people wrote in the white space on the front of the card or indeed wherever they could. There was also a highly evolved code regarding the positioning of the stamp, which could signify any number of passionate feelings.

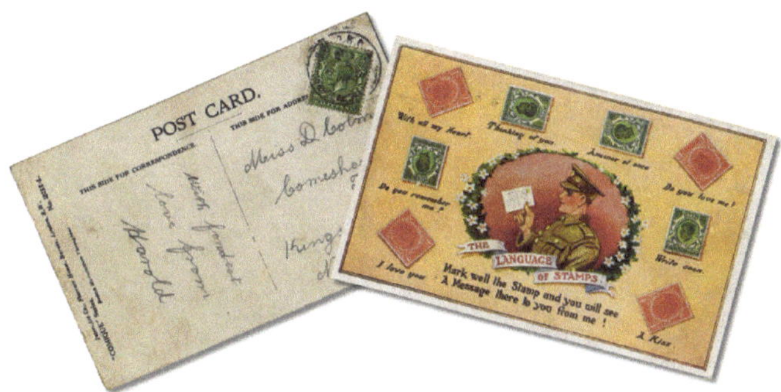

Harold sends Miss D a coded kiss

The innovation of the 'divided back', introduced in 1902, formally acknowledged that messages would be sent, regardless of the lack of privacy. Henceforth, the address would go on the right-hand side and the left-hand space could be filled with one's message of choice, from 'I'll drop in on Sunday' to a secret code or a marriage proposal.

For some collectors, the messages are the treasure, even – or especially – those banal or gloomy lines about Marjorie having a stomach upset or the rain in Rhyl. In this book my focus is on the fronts.

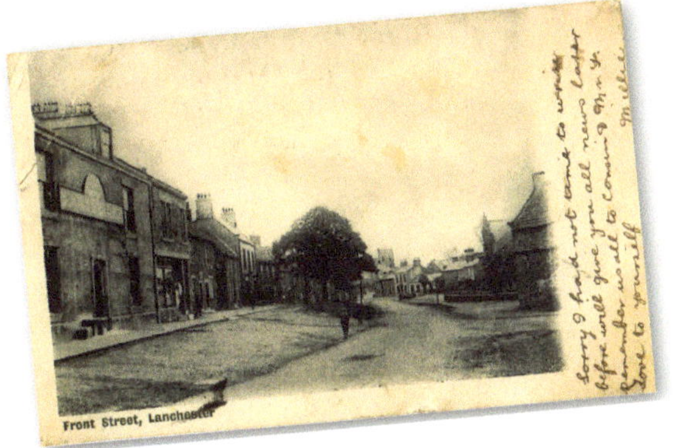

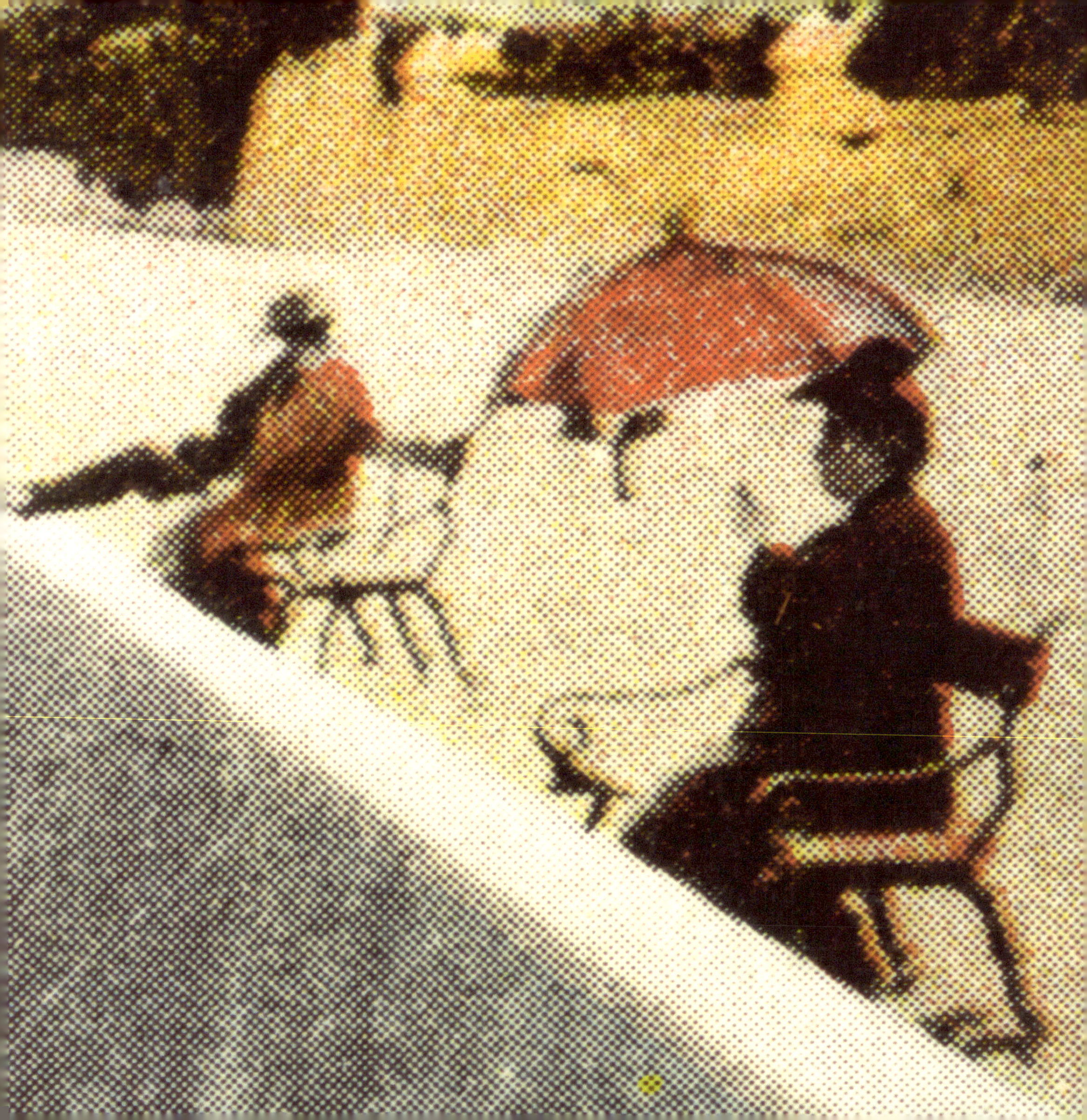

Because they so often consist of straightforward views of places, more or less busily populated (in the language of deltiologists, a postcard featuring a lot of people is 'animated'), you can use souvenir postcards to study social history: changes in fashion, transport, architecture and leisure are all reflected in their rectangular mirror. I'm fascinated by the people in postcards, more or less regardless of their date. Although some postcard photographers (particular those employed by John Hinde Studios) sometimes artfully arranged one or two people in the foreground of their shots, the better to set off the view behind them, most people in postcards are there unwittingly. The photographer set up his shot (I suspect that most postcard photographers were male in the period covered by this book – I would love to know whether there were any women photographers) and when he tripped the shutter, whoever was in the frame at that moment was captured. They're my subjects, particularly those who are not centre-stage but in the distance or at the edges.

In the 1966 film *Blow-Up*, David Hemmings' fashion photographer Thomas famously discovers clues to a murder in the enlargements he makes of photos he took in a London park. It's in the same spirit that I obsessively collect postcards with the potential to reveal secrets and then spend endless hours blowing up tiny areas of them in order to see what's 'really there'. I haven't yet uncovered a murder but, as the following pages will reveal, there *are* stories to be found. For an inveterate snooper it's addictive.

The people in postcards are rarely caught doing anything truly unexpected. For a start, the locations generally dictate the kind of activities likely to be going on – sitting, strolling and swimming, more often than not. Perhaps there might be the odd pony-trekker or cyclist. The photographers choosing when to take the shot were professionals who wouldn't waste film if there was something disrupting the scene in their viewfinder. And even if there were, the quality controllers back at the postcard company's offices would no doubt weed out any less than tranquil images. The postcard publishers were in the business of selling sunny, peaceful shots of places at their best, so that in turn tourists would buy them to reflect well on their choice of holiday. It feels like a small miracle, then, to find something 'unexpected' that slipped through the process and made it into print (I won't spoil the surprise of my best finds, revealed later in these pages). Let me be absolutely honest: more often than not, the people in the tiny scenes I've isolated in these postcards and homed in on, *Blow-Up* style, are not doing

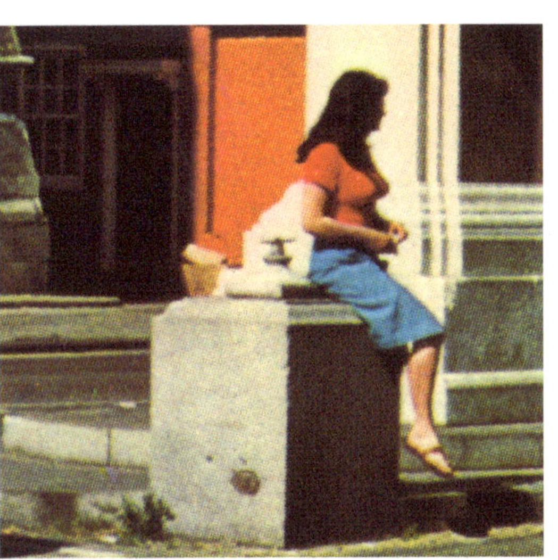

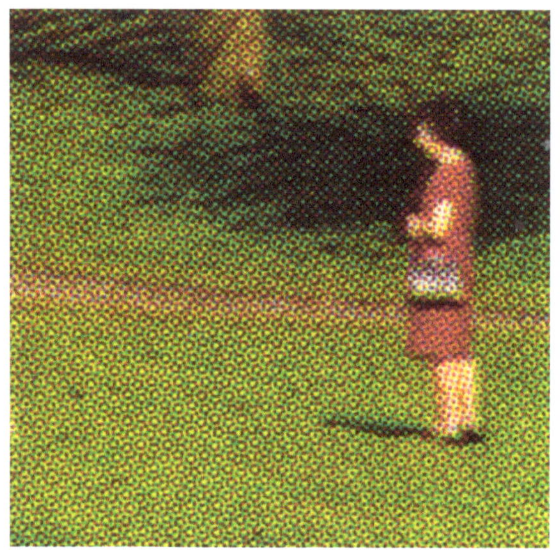

all day crouched in Snoopers Paradise in the North Laine going through postcards). So it pays to develop an efficient eye when appraising postcards for their hidden potential. Take this French postcard, for instance.

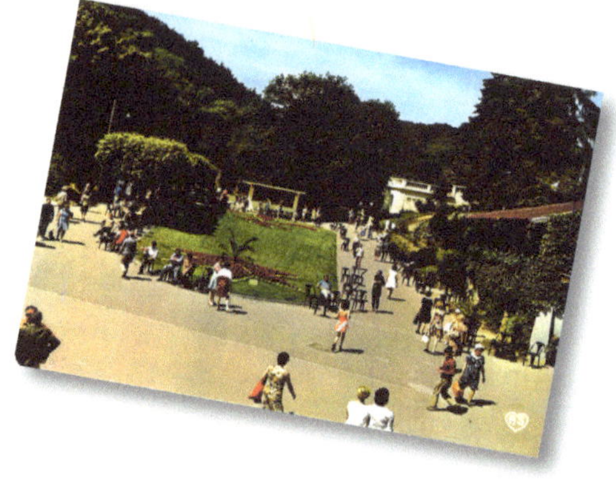

anything out of the ordinary in the context of the scene but let's say they may have an air of mystery about them that encourages storytelling. The most potent characteristic is isolation, someone who manages to seem magnificently – or tragically – alone, even in a crowded place. Or there may be an interaction in progress – a conversation or heads turning – is it an assignation, or a row? Was that the moment when two people fell in love? Well, most likely not, but it has pleased me to imagine that it might have been.

When I'm looking through boxes of postcards in junkshops – the typical location for most of my finds – I have to see quickly, if that's possible. More than once I've made myself quite unwell from spending hours bent over boxes of postcards (a condition known in our household as 'hassocks' from the station just outside Brighton where I once had to get off the train home because I was so crippled with stomach ache after spending

While my eye may be caught, initially, by a solitary figure in the busy park, it's always worth looking

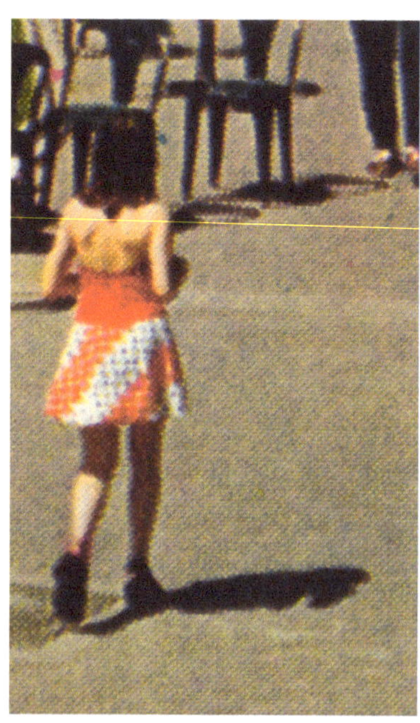

harder – then I might see the two men down in the bottom left corner, red-faced and sweaty: are they having an argument? What about?

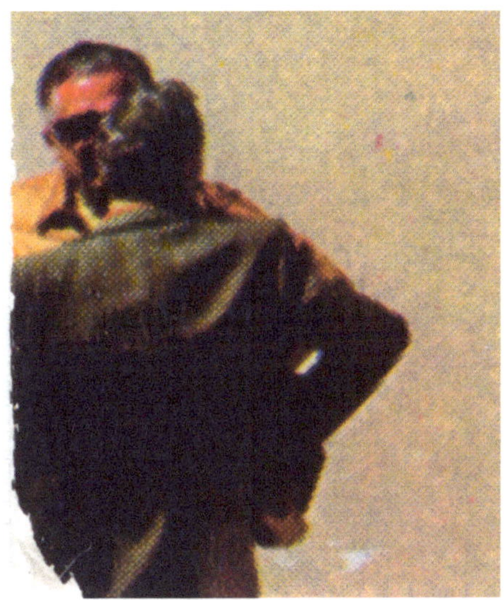

I'm onto something! But it's only by virtue of looking harder still that I might notice the woman with her leg in plaster which, while not of earth-shattering significance, is nonetheless unusual for a postcard.

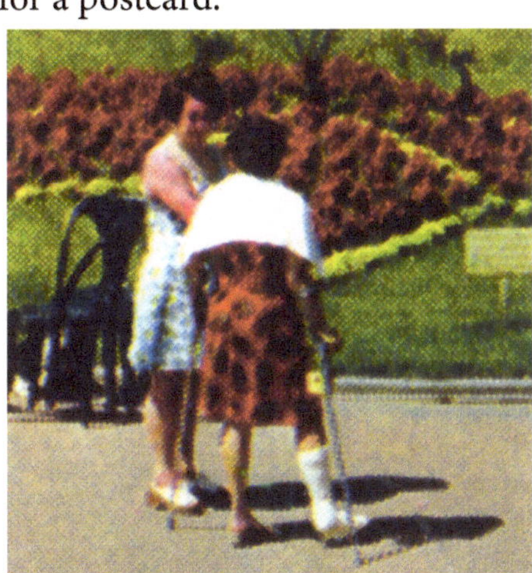

I want to call the people I zoom in on in postcards 'hidden'. That isn't literally the case – or very rarely. They're not usually so small you can't see them with the naked eye, but the fact is that you have to look at a postcard in an almost perverse way in order to see past what the photographer intended you to see and to notice the more interesting scenes on the

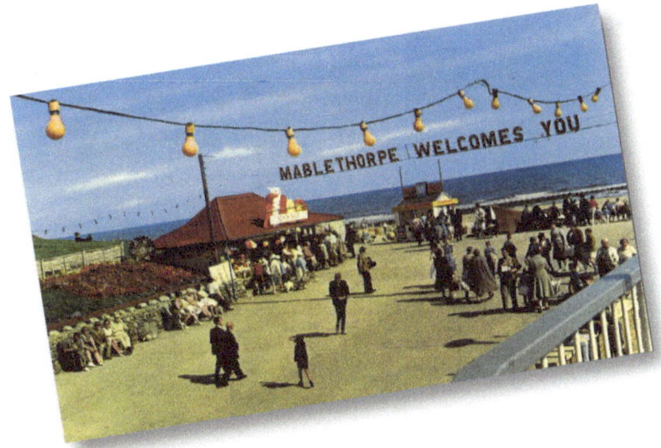

sidelines. So with this postcard of Mablethorpe, the diagrammatic relationship between the four people in the centre of the shot is intriguing – why are they all in black? Who is the impossibly tall boy?

But then I notice that two other men are

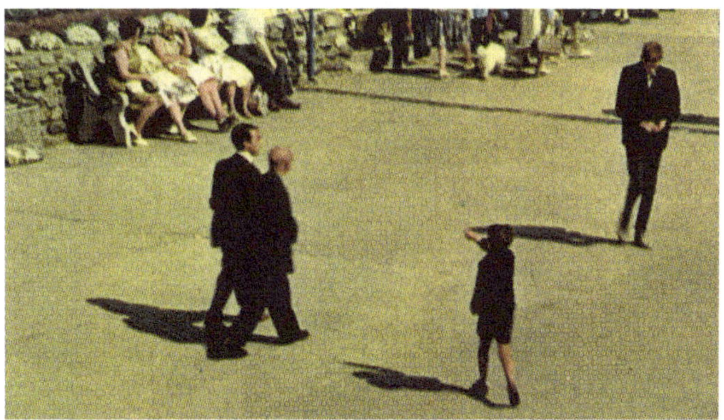

both in distinctive striped jackets and seem to be carrying bulky objects in front of them. What's going on with them?

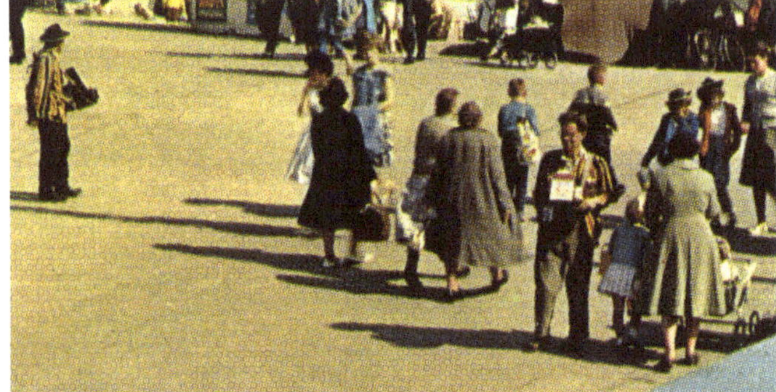

Finally, I notice the boy lounging on the grass above the prom and he's the one who I find the most engaging, whose story I'd like to imagine.

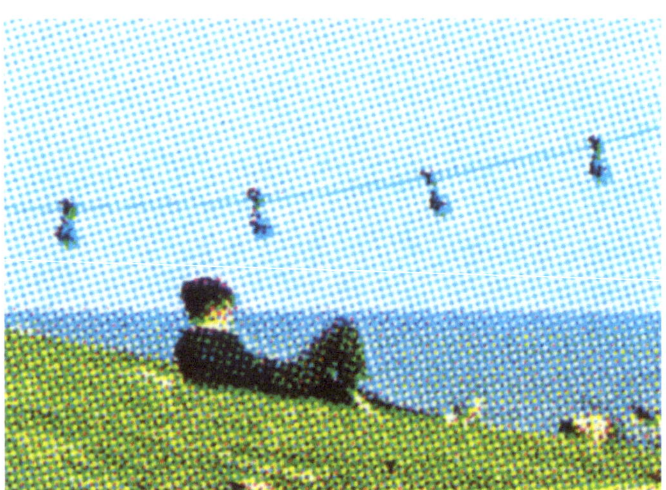

There are plenty of people who I'll show you in this book that you might not otherwise have noticed, but perhaps only one who was almost invisible from the start (see the image to the right).

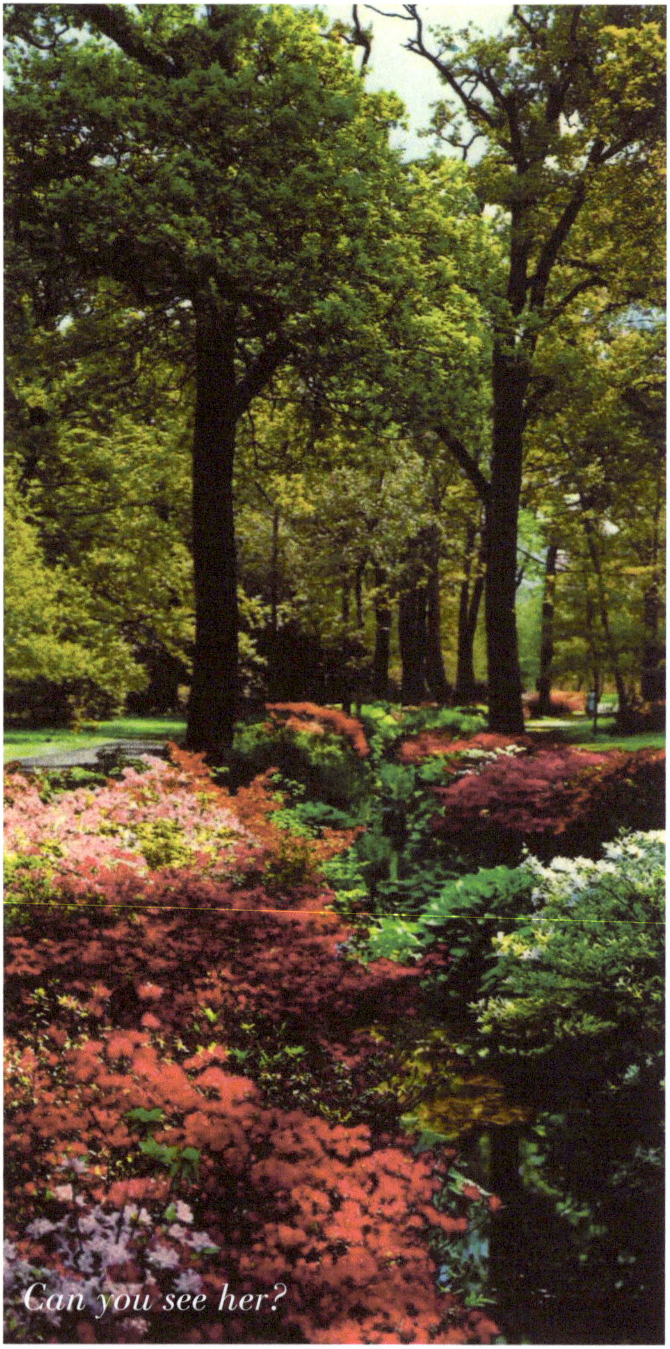

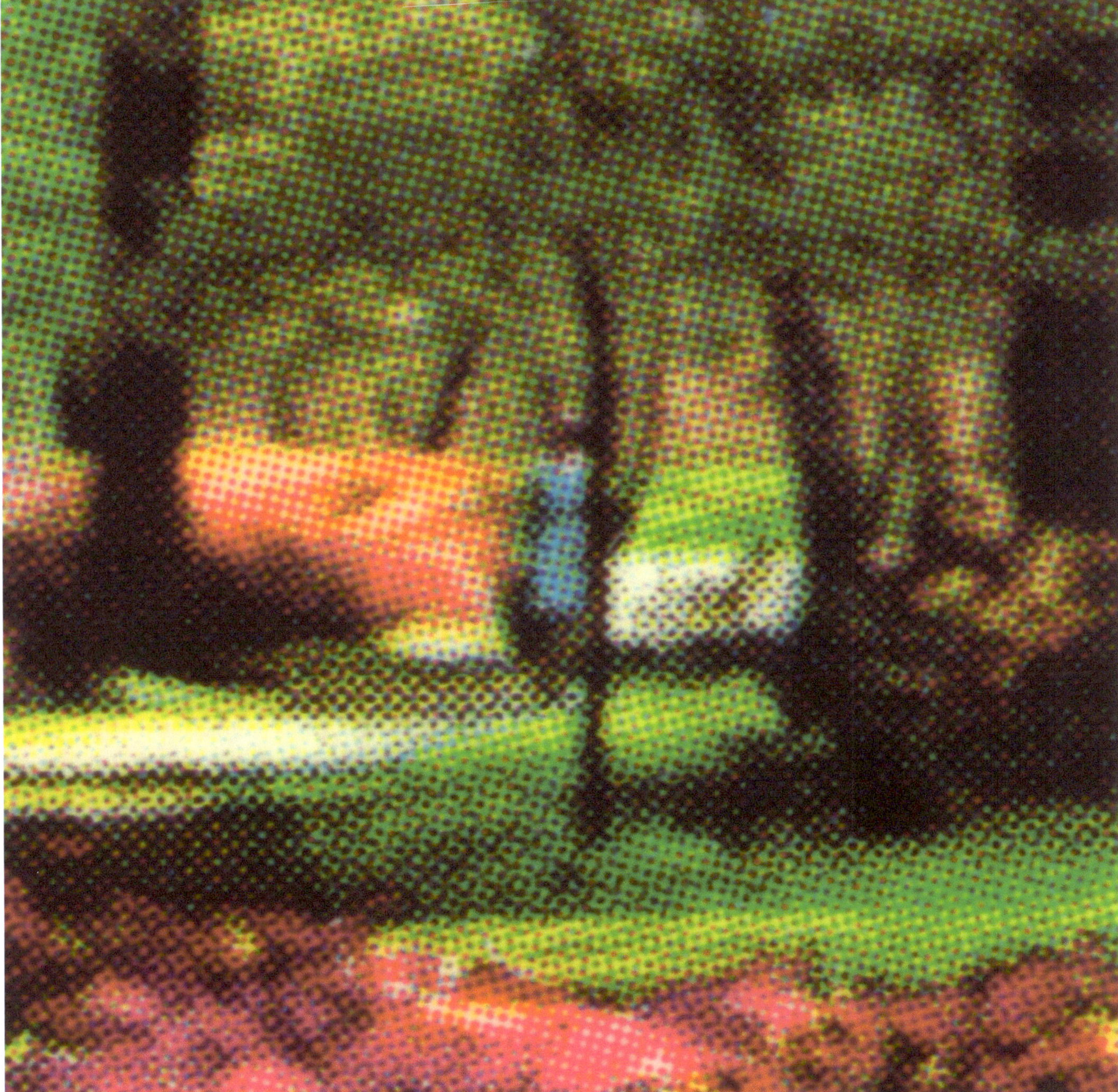

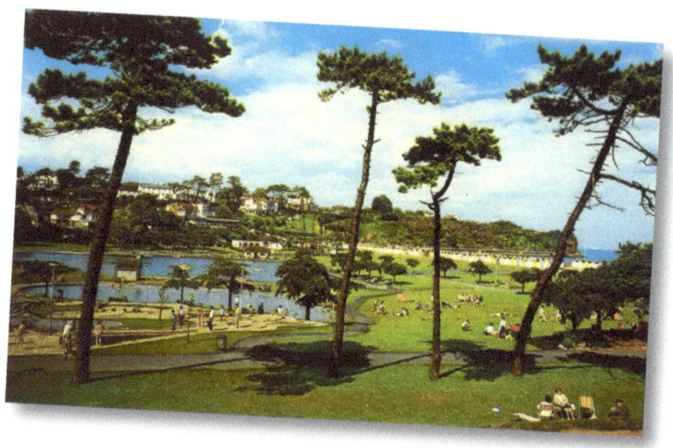

I like people whose noses and toes encroach into the rectangle of the postcard from the invisible world beyond its edges. They are the markers of the photographer's decision as to how to frame his shot, how much world to include. For the photographer, the centre of the card (or perhaps the central but artfully off-centre area) is usually the most important part of the image, but I prefer the periphery. The periphery is often where you'll find children running blurrily away from their minders, miserable couples, or, much better, people seeming to catch sight of each other for the first time and liking what they see. It helps that I have a very active imagination, making me think there's longing or loathing, mockery or even madness behind every interaction I witness. But in this book I can indulge my tendency to see stories in everything without restraint. Indeed, it's the stories that transform the almost certainly very ordinary and blameless individuals who were

The position of people matters in a postcard. It's a small canvas, into which an almost infinite amount of space can be squeezed (as in the card above). I'm particularly drawn to the figures on the edges of the cards, especially if they've been cut off. Those two men arguing in the French park would not endear themselves to me so much if they weren't trapped in the very corner of the card.

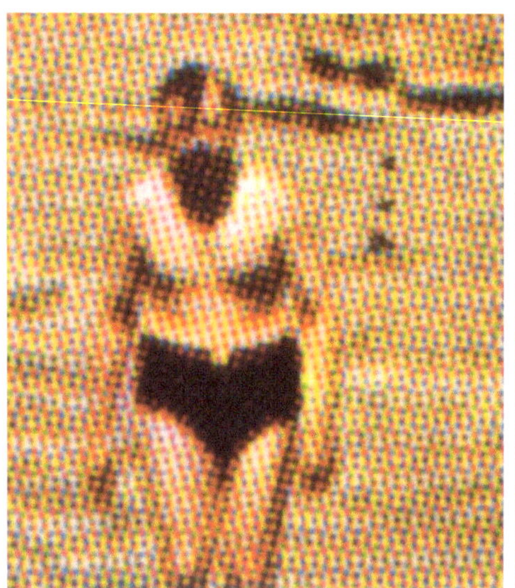

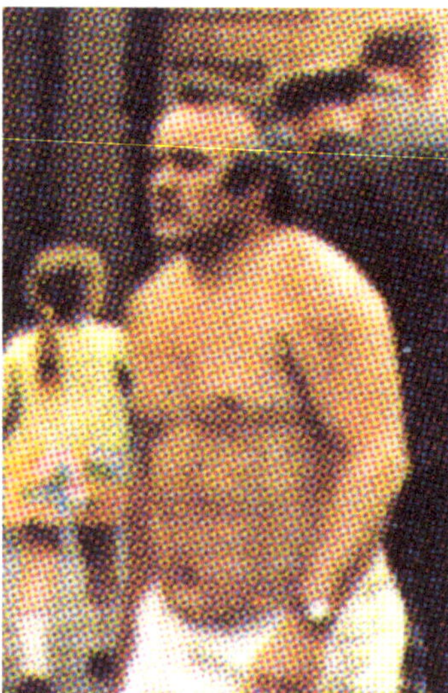

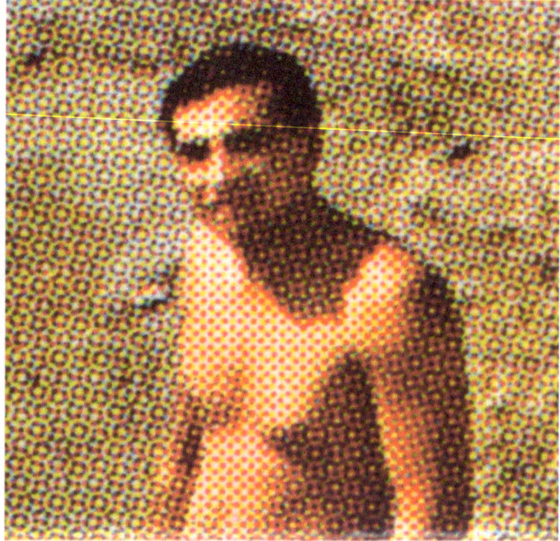

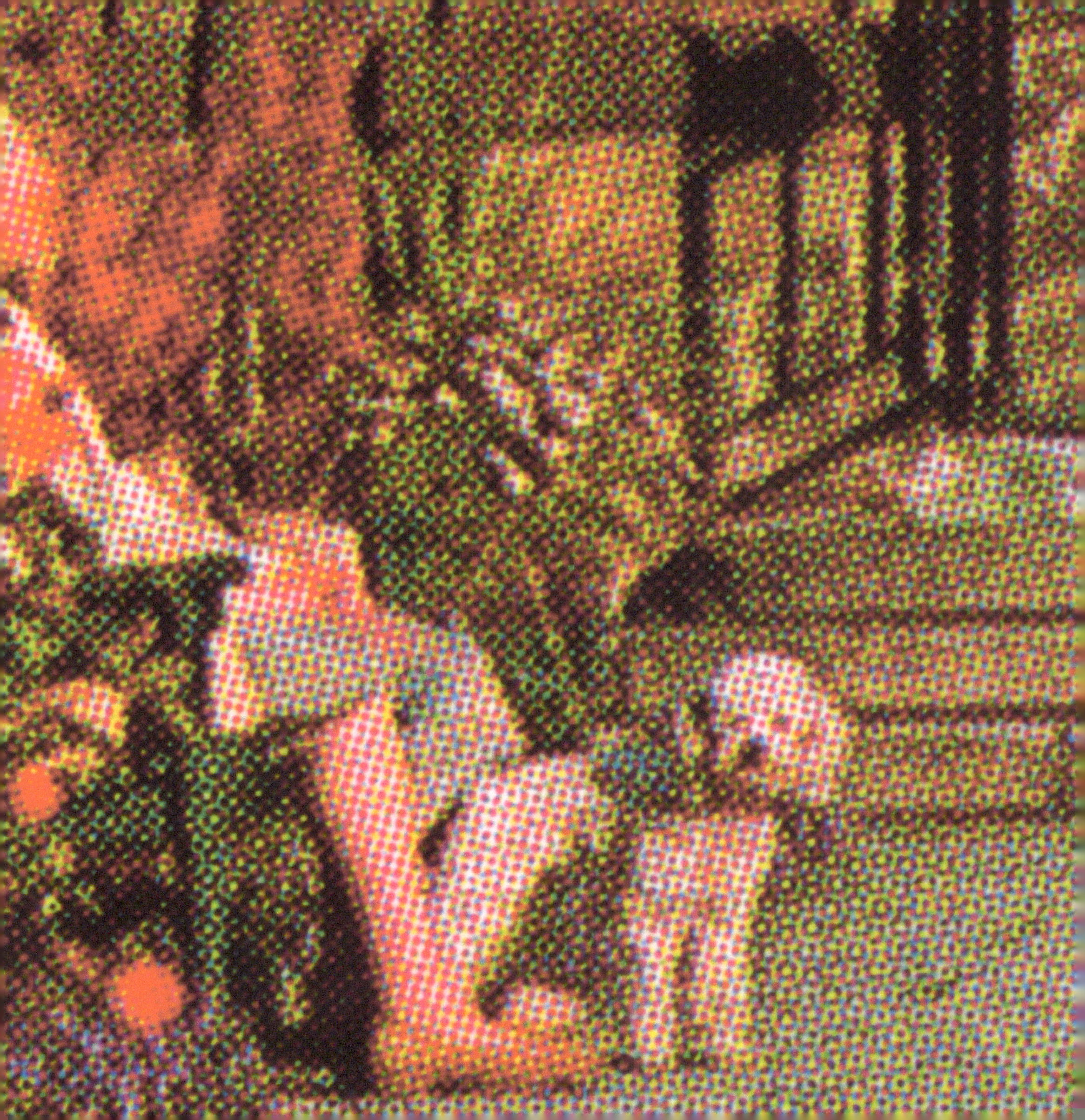

unwittingly caught on camera into the actors in tiny dramas, so go with me when I see, I don't know, kidnappers on the beach, escaped convicts in the park or runaways at the shopping centre.

There's another detail that I look out for in postcards. It's when someone in the scene interacts in some way with elements that have been added to the card during the design process. To illustrate, in the card on the right, a young woman is paddling in the sea at Port Erin on the Isle of Man. The card is overprinted with its location and thus the young woman has ended up stamped with

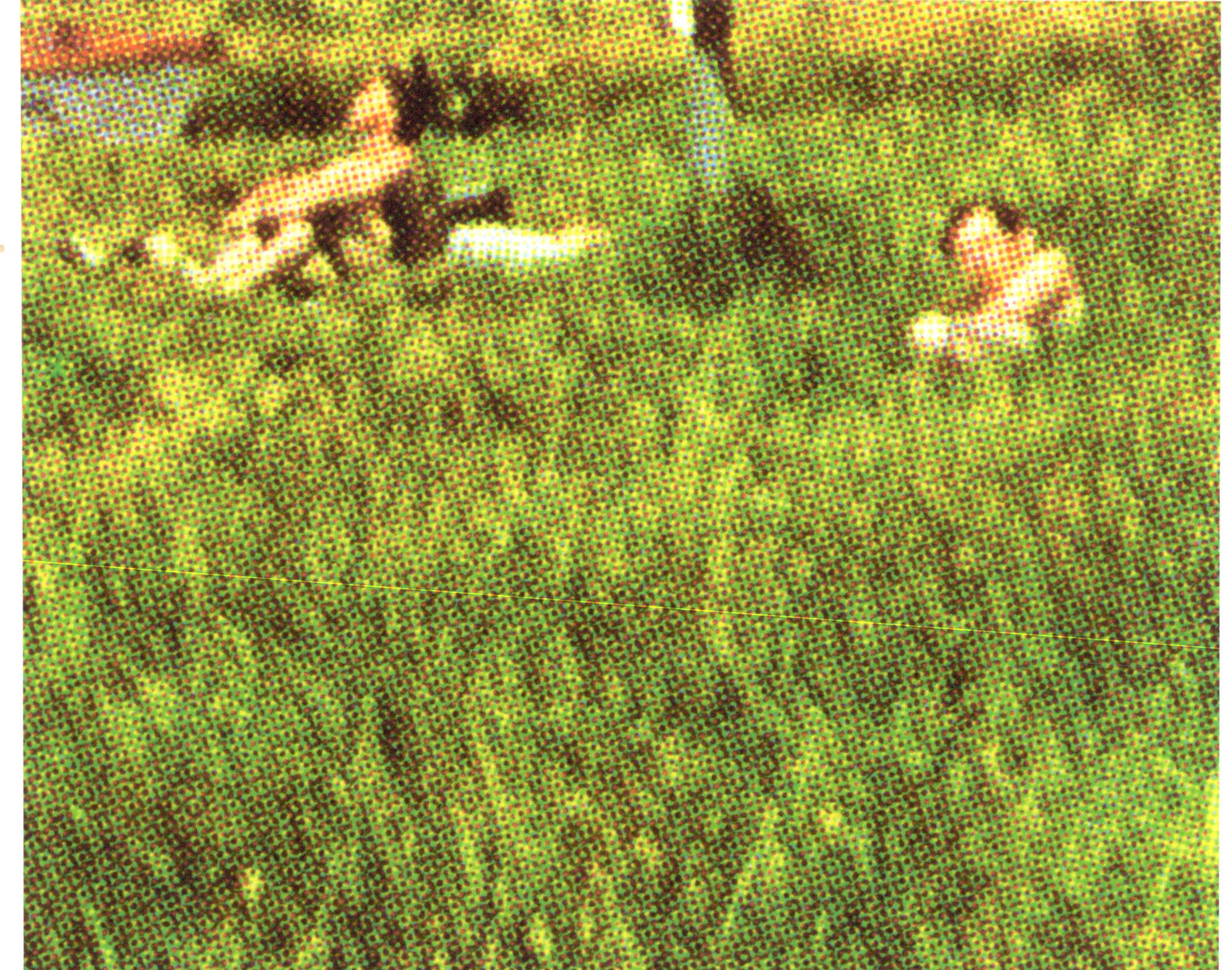

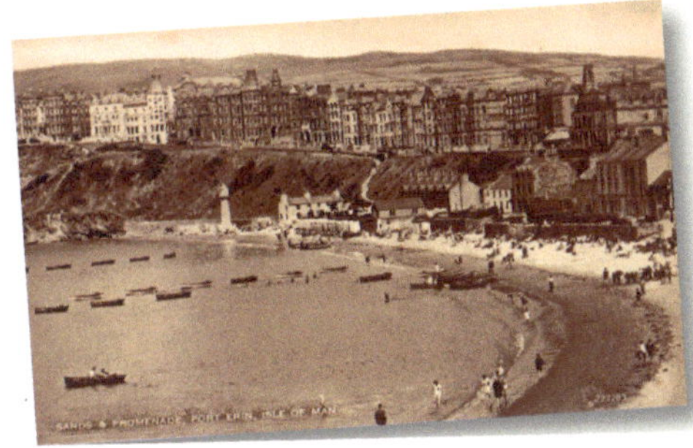

'MAN' – does she perhaps have men on her mind? – and there is a young man conveniently standing just nearby.

The very act of enlargement is transformative. When you blow up most printed images, they break down into their constituent dots, becoming instant Lichtensteins and, as such, enormously appealing. There's a poignancy in the reversing of the illusion that allows printed pinpricks of pink, yellow, blue and black to look remarkably like real life: when you break the spell by showing how the trick's done, it undermines our certainty that photographs are 'real'. All is evanescent: beautiful but insubstantial. Then reality wobbles a little too.

Some postcards, especially older ones, weren't printed using offset lithography but are actual photographs and so don't break down into dots, but these have a different quality when enlarged, like a painting (see the bottom image).

Here, then, are ordinary people caught unawares, tiny moments in unknown lives, some of them intended wto be enjoyed just for themselves, others spun into stories. Soon we won't send postcards any more, so this is my tribute to a beloved art form.

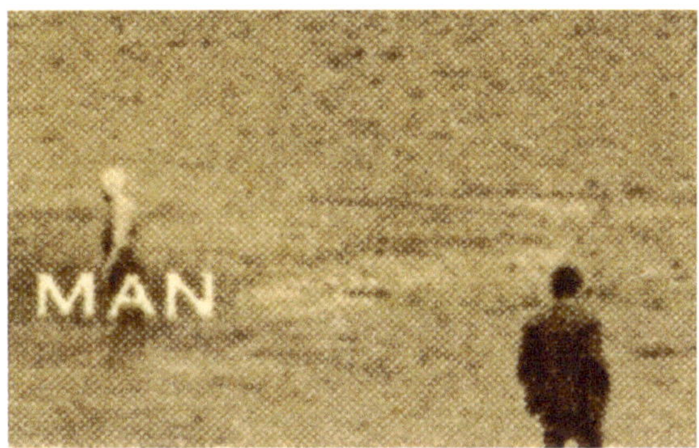

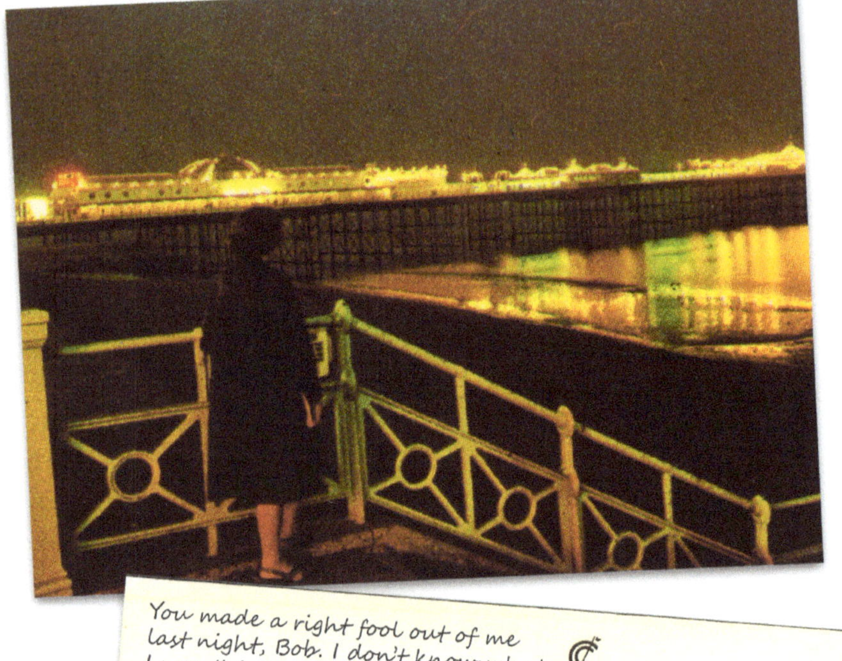

BRIGHTON

You made a right fool out of me last night, Bob. I don't know what I was thinking, going along with yet another of your harebrained schemes. I waited for your friend Colin, like you said, at the top of the steps along from the Pier – the Palace Pier. I suppose I should have known he wouldn't show up, and I'd told the other girls I was going on a date too. Was that your idea of a joke, Bob? Because it wasn't funny, standing there for what felt like an age, ignoring all the rude comments and fending off horrible teddy boys. I won't fall for one of your silly tricks again. I suppose I'll see you in the Star and Garter as usual on Saturday.
Dot

Brighton by night

Published by COASTAL CARDS Ltd. Holland-on-Sea

VITA NOVA

PRINTED IN HOLLAND

Mr R. WARD
2 Simons Rd
BECKTON
London E6

PS: You won't be getting a stick of rock from me this year, Bob, that's for sure.

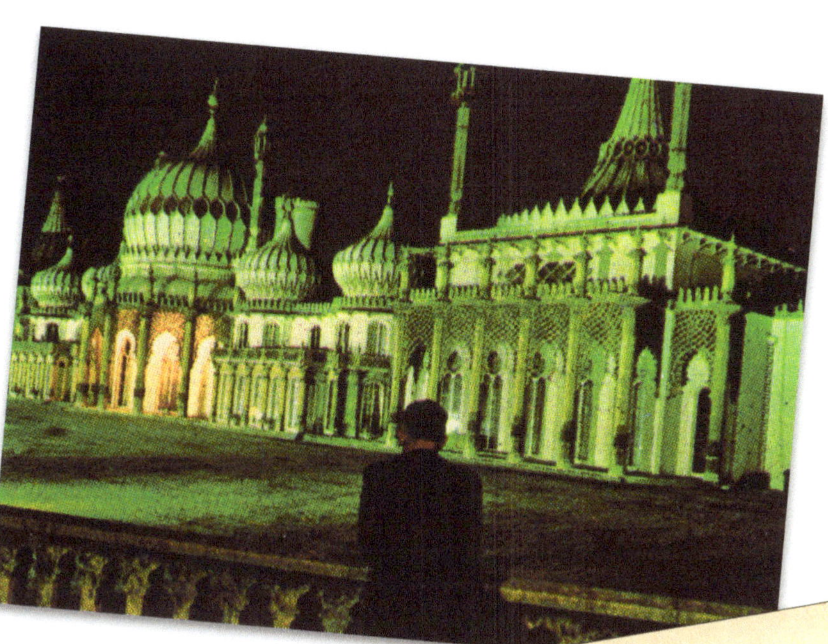

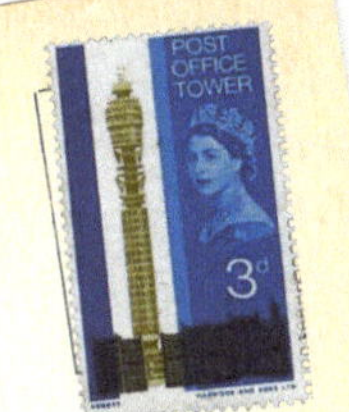

Dear Bob,
A quick line from Brighton. That girl you said you'd set me up with never turned up last night. What was she called, Dotty? I think she must have been dotty because I waited in the cold for hours and she never showed her face. You said to wait by the Dome at seven and she'd come along and we could take it from there. Well, nothing doing, my friend. I felt a right mug, but then a drunk bird toppled off her heels just nearby and I went to give her a hand and... let's just say, it turned out all right.

See you next week at the office, you old pimp,
Col

FISA - Great Britain - LONDON

Golden Shield

BRIGHTON, Sussex

Printed in Spain

Bob Ward

c/o Breandon's & Co

Longton Road

Beckton

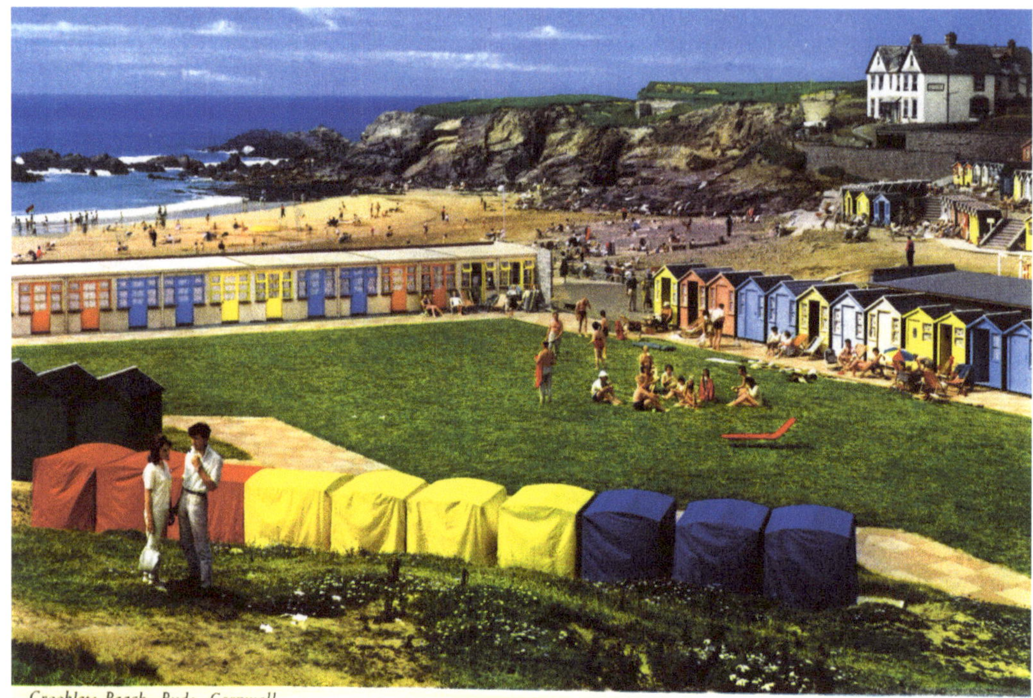

Crooklets Beach, Bude, Cornwall.

Photo: E. Ludwig, John Hinde Studios.

BUDE

"Are you sure he said he'd give us ten bob?"

"That's what he said."

"Ten bob between us or ten bob each?"

"I dunno. I didn't like to ask."

"Me neither, it would've seemed rude. But I could do with ten bob."

"Me too."

"I only came down here to fetch my bag."

"He said we weren't to talk, just 'look romantic.'"

"Well, that's rich. Anyway, he's still messing about with his camera. What do they call that prop thing?'

"A tripod."

"And did he really say he was called Ludwig? What kind of name is that? It sounds German."

"Well he has a German accent so I guess he must be."

"He's a Hun! My Dad won't like that."

"Your Dad doesn't know the War's been over for nearly thirty years."

"Oh he knows all right, he just can't pretend everything's all nice again with them Germans."

"Silly old…"

"Don't you start on my Dad! If I hadn't left my bag here last night I wouldn't be within a mile of you."

"Look, he's telling us to shut up, he's flapping his hands to say calm down."

"No he isn't, he's just saying be patient. He's still messing with his camera. Must be worth a fortune, that thing."

"Anyway, sorry about last night. Do you forgive me?"

"Do I forgive you for kissing Margaret Keane? No, I do not."

"I'd had a few too many. She threw herself at me."

"Did she now? Well she's just over there showing off her wares in a deckchair, so I'll ask her about it in a minute. As soon as matey here's finished with us."

"Oh, no, Sal, don't make a scene."

"I'll make a scene if I want to. You bloody deserve it. I swore blind last night that was the end of it. You've messed up once too often, Peter Sykes. Can't hold your liquor. Can't keep your hands to yourself."

"Sal, you look so pretty today. Don't be mad at me."

"I know what you're doing. I can feel you stroking my arm. Don't think that's going to do the trick."

"Look, he's ready. Stop talking. I'll walk you back to your digs after this. I'll buy you a ninety-nine."

"You really think that's all it'll take?"

"Ssh, he's taking his picture."

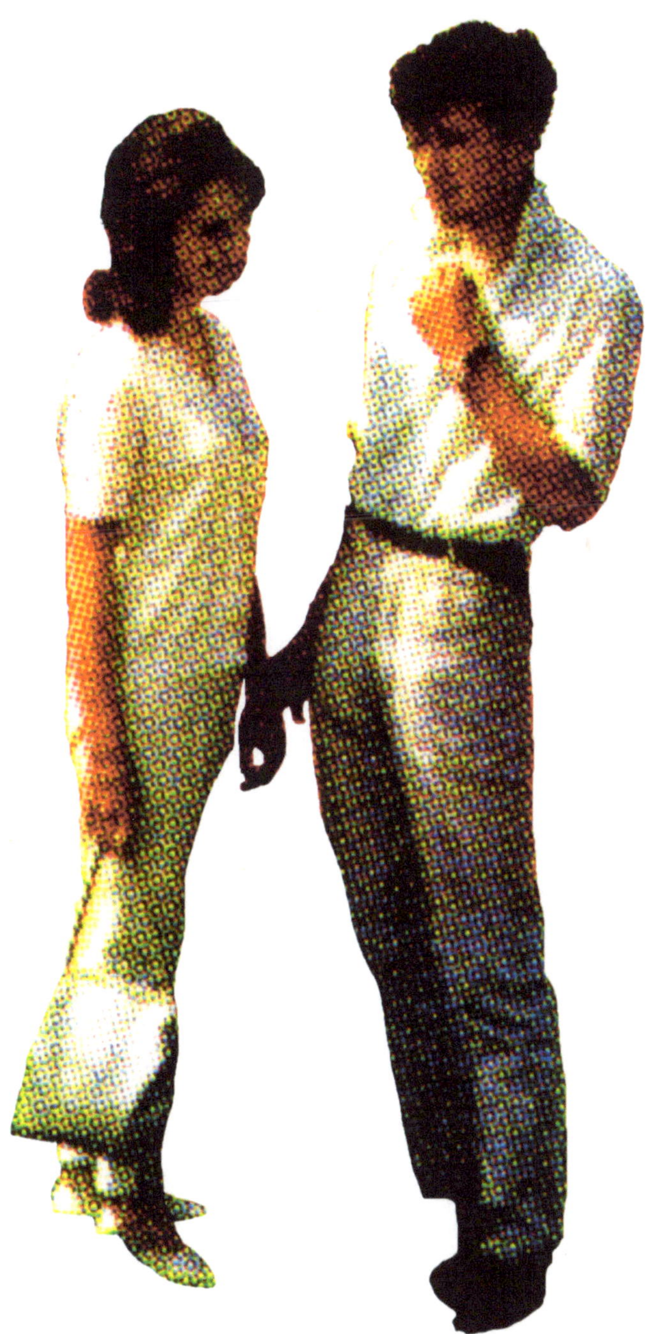

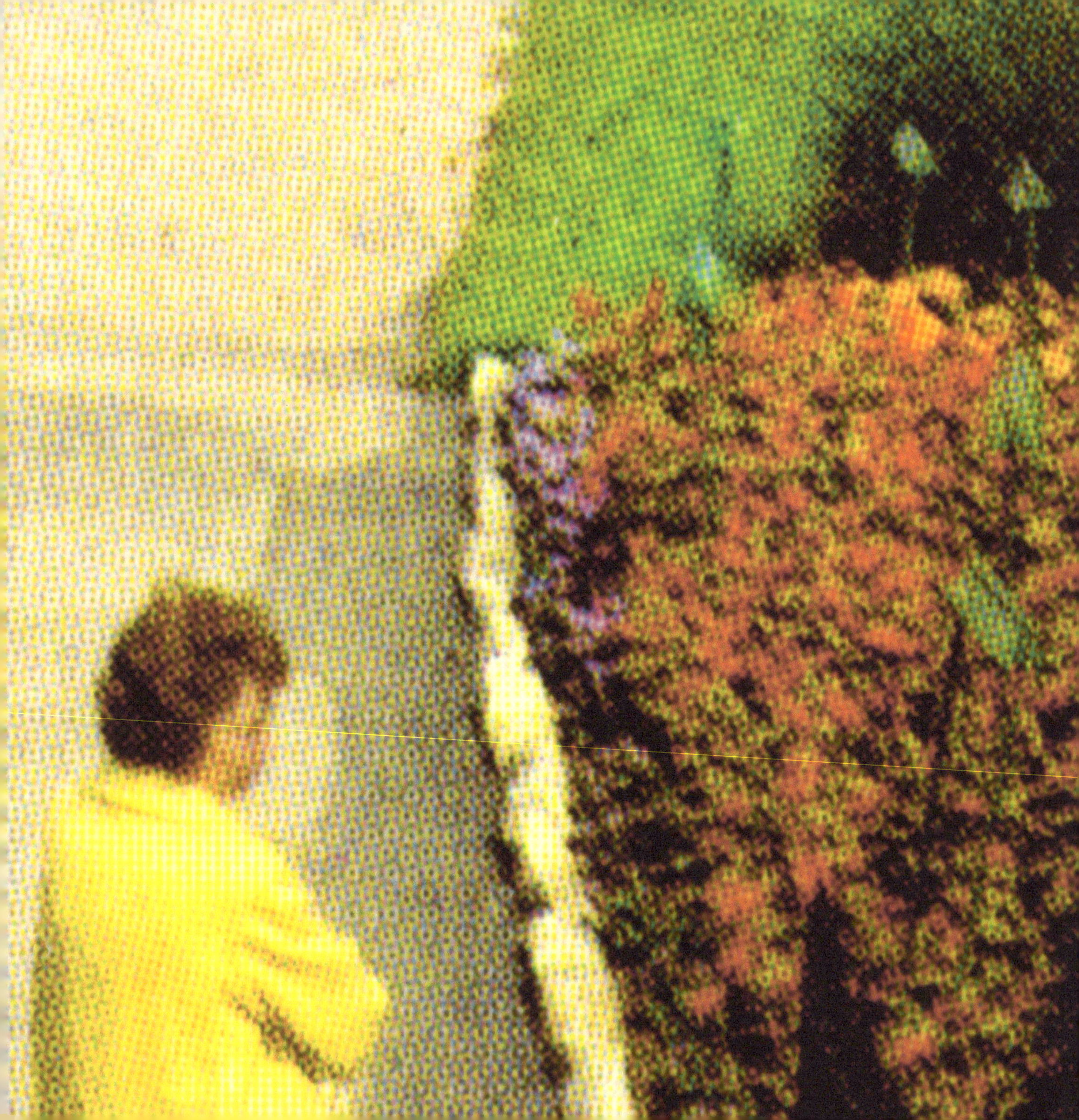

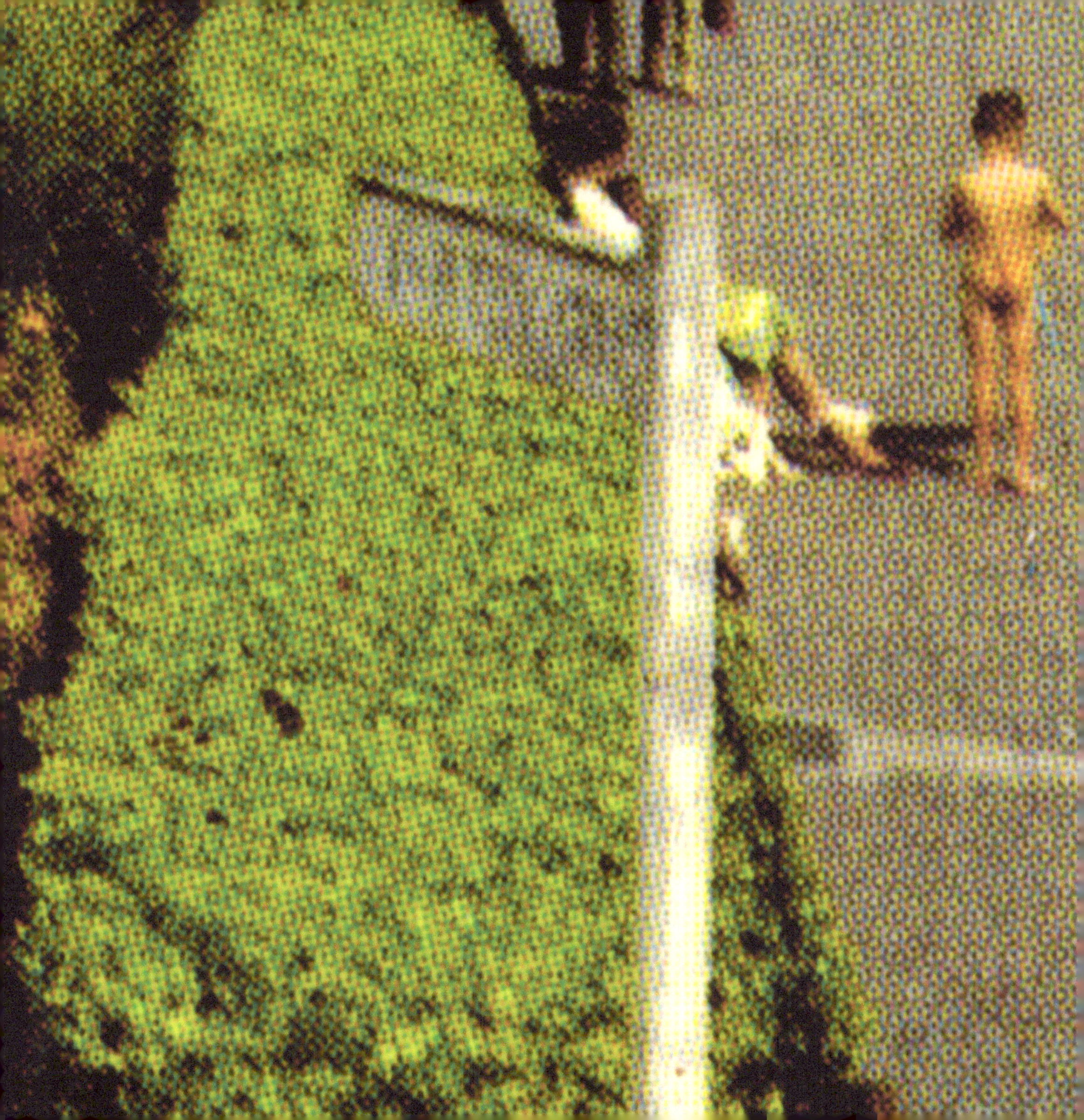

BROAD HAVEN

"Do you see, away up there, boy, they're building a path right around Wales, the Coast Path. It's been in the making for about ten years now, ever since they set up the National Park. There's a fellow I've had the honour of meeting, name of Ronald Lockley, he's all about Wales, he is – the land, the birds, the seals. Writes books about them. His latest one's about the rabbits. But it's the birds, really, that set him apart. They're an absolute passion with him. I went to a talk he gave, in Cardiff, all about gannets and shearwaters and puffins and the like. Inspirational, it was. He used to live on an island, behind us to the South, Skokholm Island, just him and his wife and the birds and rabbits. He's written the most marvellous books about it. I shook his hand afterwards, after the talk. He had the grip of a true countryman. I'll never forget it.

"Are you listening, Robert? It's thanks to him that they're making the path right around the coast and one day soon, you and me, we'll be able to stride along it together. What's that? No, I don't think Mummy will be up to it. It'll be something for you and me to do together. Imagine it, setting out along that shining path, past the cliffs and the bays, the sea sparkling and the seagulls crying. Oh, it'll be marvellous. I cannot wait.

"They're forging their way around the whole of our country, brooking no opposition. Sod the landowners – oh, don't tut so, Robert – yes, sod them, they're all Little Englanders anyway. They're building us a path right around the beloved country and then we can march all around it for the first time – like beating the bounds that they did in the old days.

"I read about the progress they're making quite regularly in the paper, which section they're on, what they're having to do to forge ever onwards: bridges and steps and stiles. It's like Hannibal crossing the Alps. When was that, Robert, do you know?

"No, it was not during the Winter Olympics. Good God, boy, do they teach you nothing at that school? The Second Punic War, two hundred and eighteen BC. The elephants, lad, the elephants. It's glorious military history. When we get back home, I'll find you a book about it.

"Yes, we'll come back as soon as that path is ready to welcome us. Maybe we'll even bring a tent with us and camp. Imagine that, a father and his boy, heating stew in a billy can and singing songs of yore.

"Yes, I can see her coming. I hope she's got us some decent sandwiches in that bag. And potato crisps. Welsh cakes, maybe, for afters? I hope she managed to get the tea good and hot in the Thermos. Can't stand it lukewarm. Go on then, Robert, run and help her if you're so inclined."

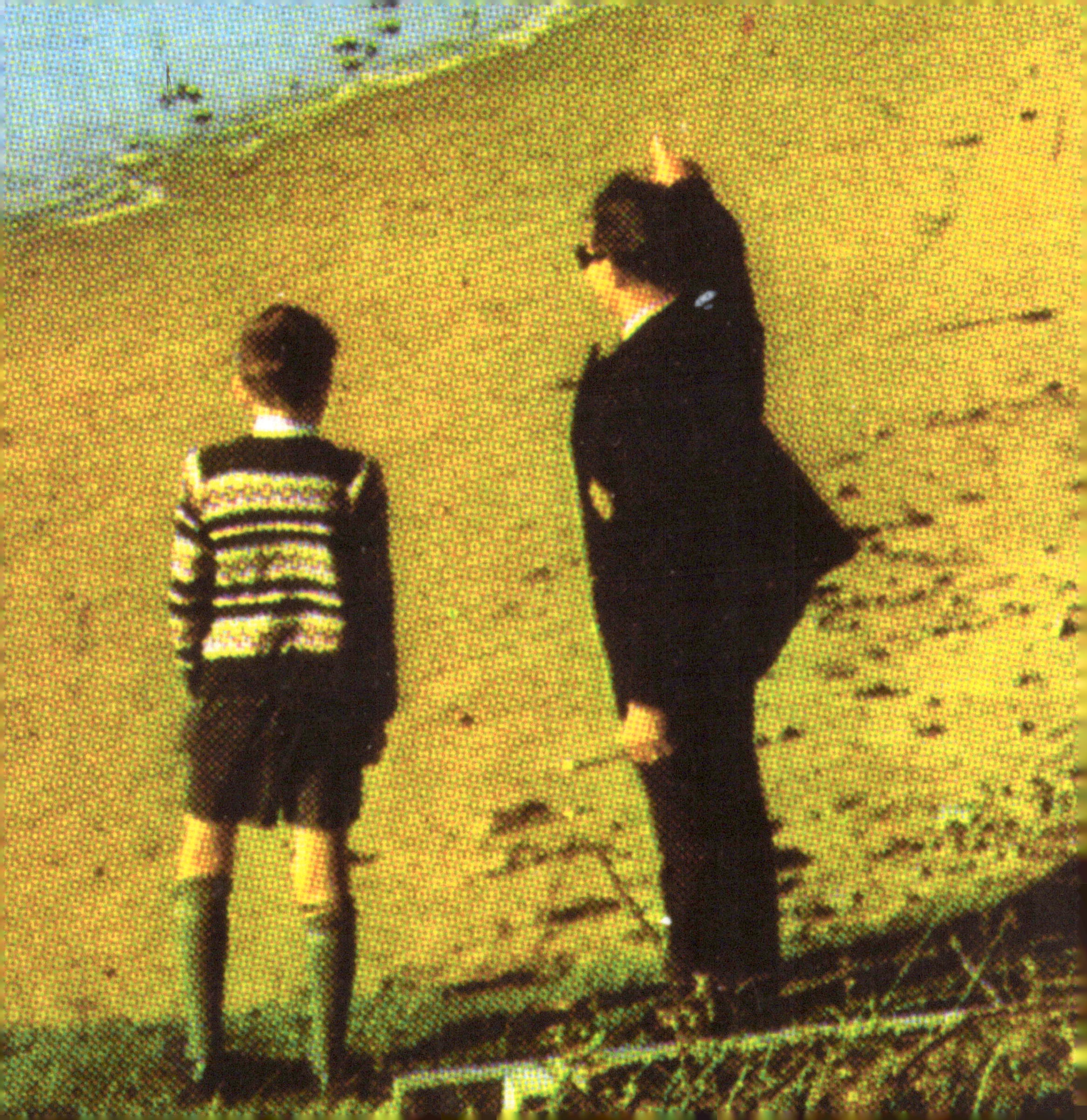

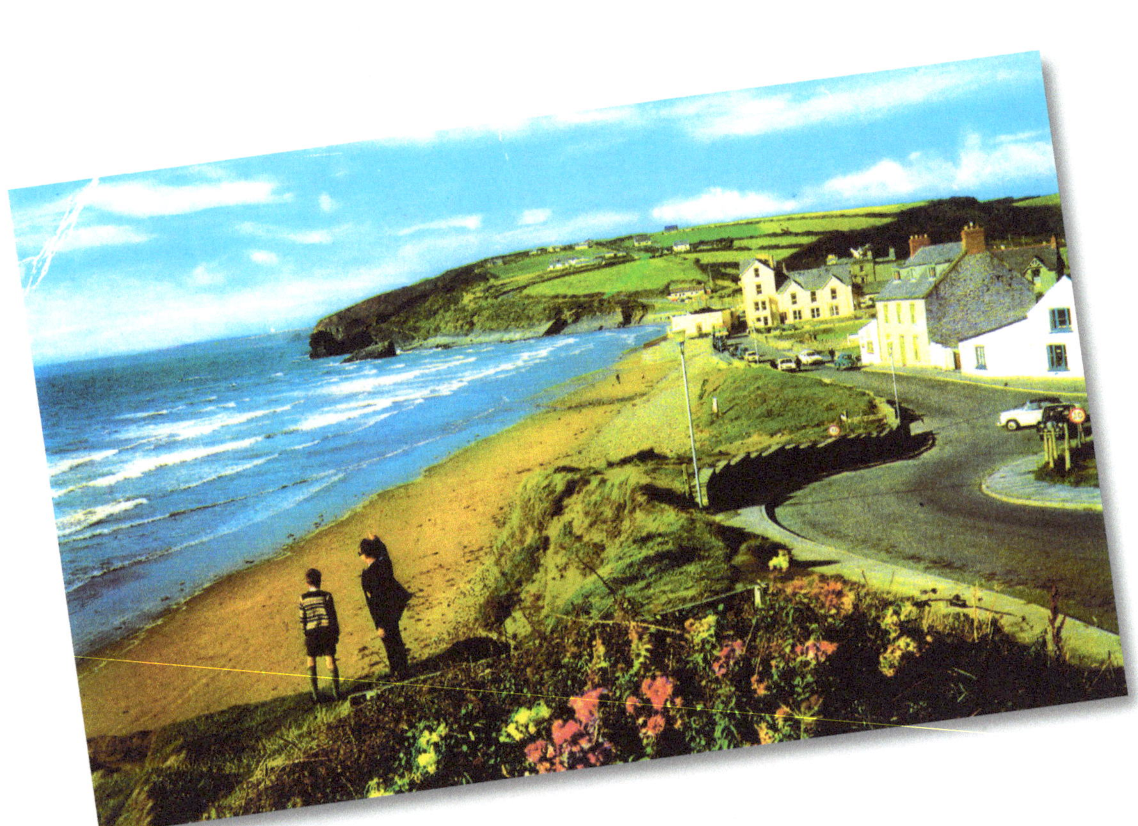

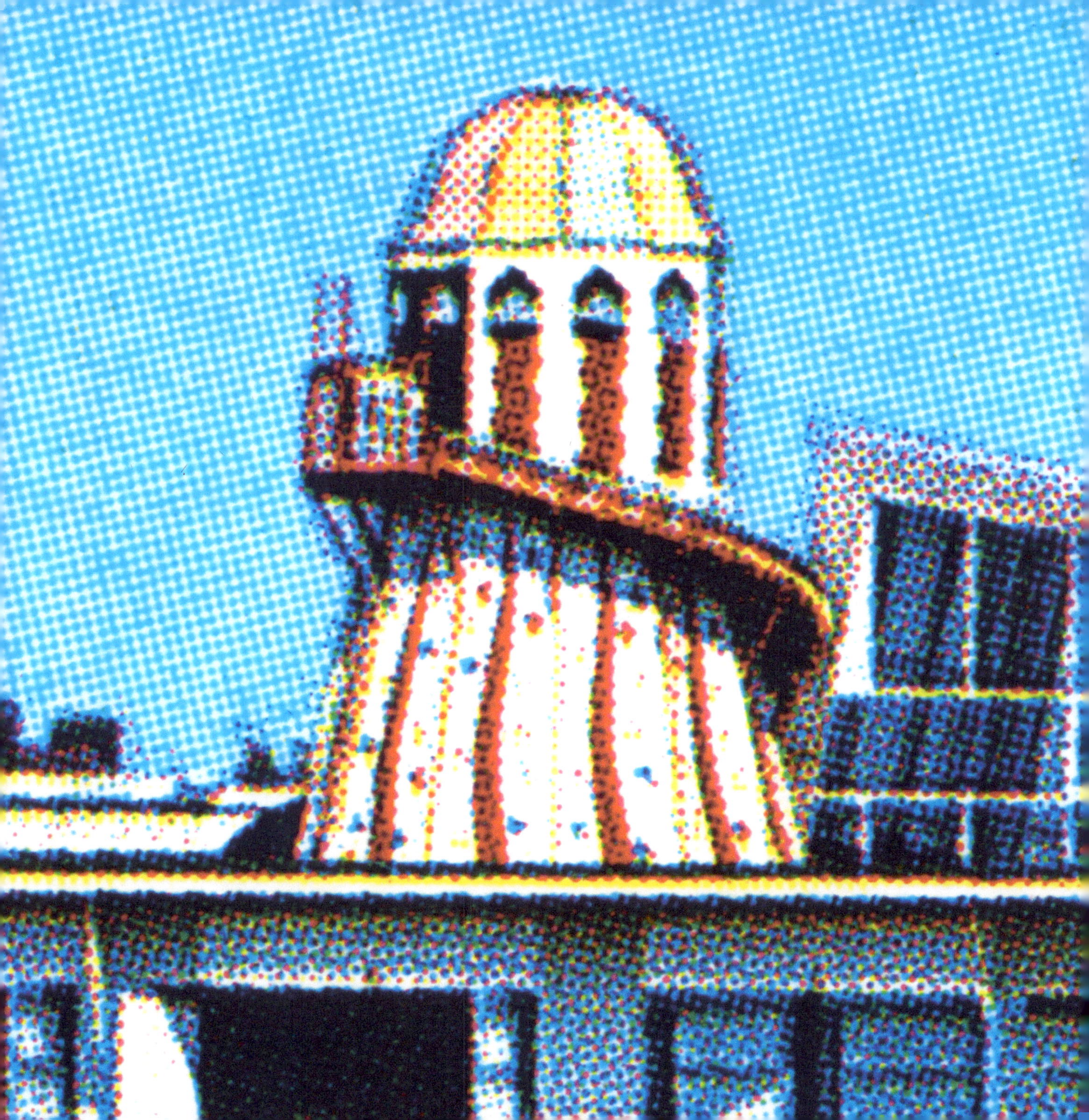

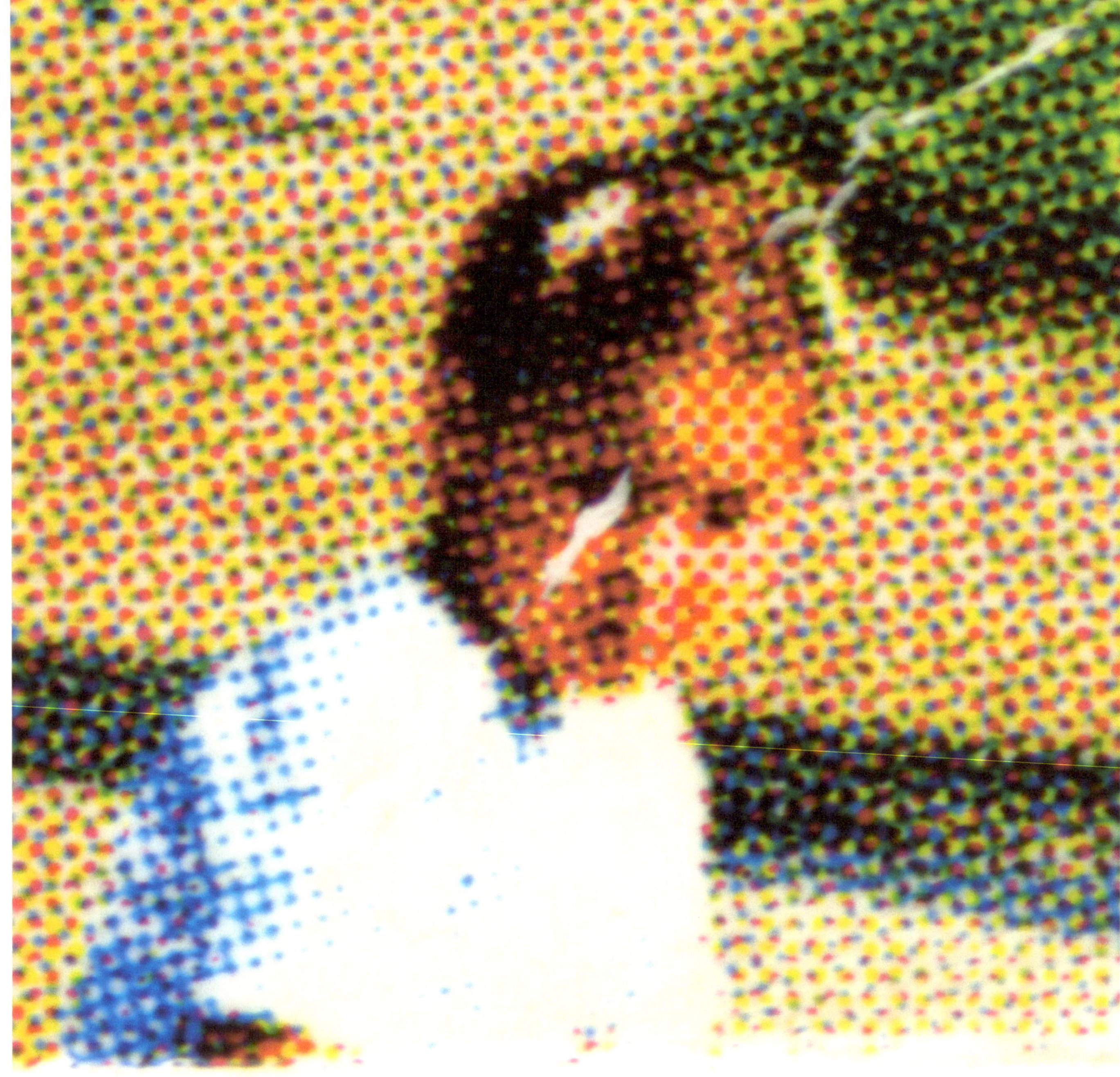

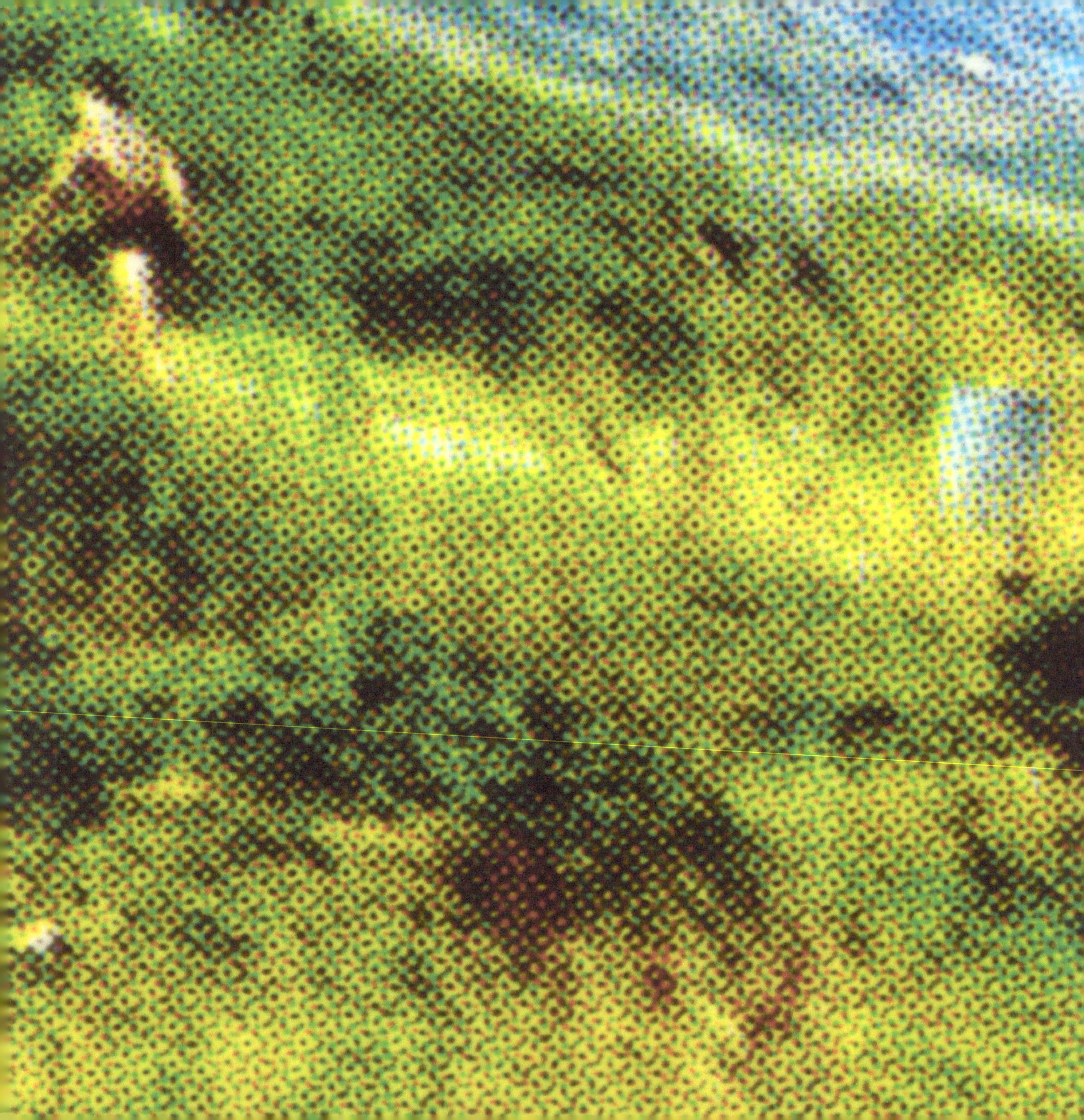

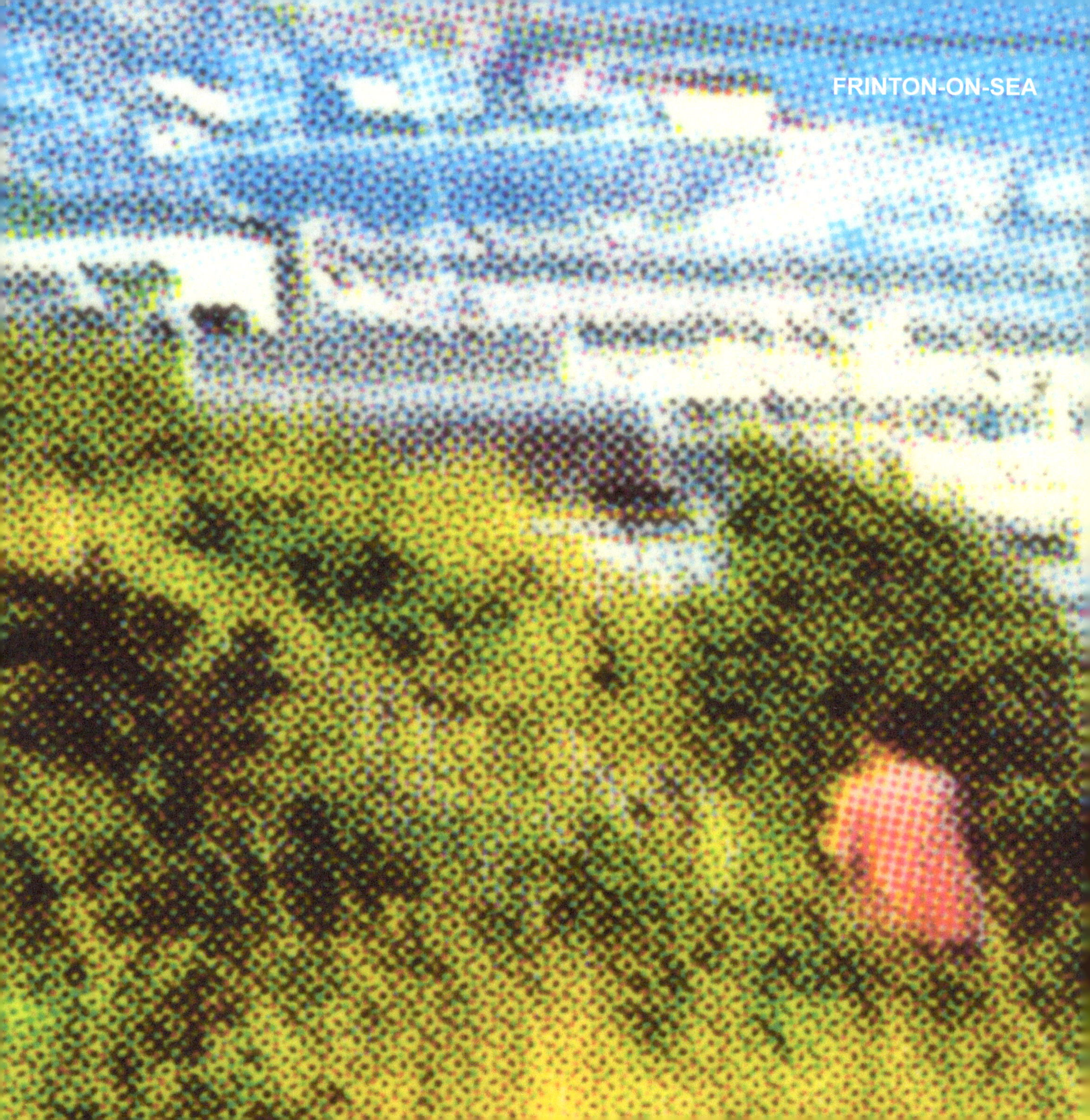
FRINTON-ON-SEA

Oh Mouse, Mouse, please stop. Don't run away like this. I'm so sorry. I made a bad call.

She's striding away ahead of me up the path. She hasn't even got changed. Mousie, you'll catch cold. If only I hadn't fallen prey to that moment in the water. It was just a moment and I couldn't resist her lovely tanned arms in the sunshine, the water shining on them like jewels.

What will we do when we get back to the B&B? It's going to be ghastly. I suppose she won't want to share a room any more. She'll probably insist on catching the train home straight away – and then what will she say to everyone? "Oh, Margaret tried to kiss me while we were swimming"? Maybe not. It'll all be brushed under the carpet like so much else, but we'll never be the same, will we? That's what I can't bear.

"Mouse! Mousie! Please stop!"

No, she's not going to stop. I think my lungs are going to burst if I don't catch my breath. I want to stop and go through what happened moment by moment, so that I'll remember it – I don't ever want to forget it, in spite of everything – and to try to work out how I got it so wrong. But I can't stop, I need to get back to the room before she can pack up and leave.

"Mouse!"

I suppose I got my hopes up when she agreed to come down here with me. But then again, it was just a week in Frinton and who doesn't share a room when they go on holiday with their friend? She'll think I've taken advantage of her terribly. Specially with me being that little bit older. Oh I wish she wouldn't call me "Mummy" the way she does sometimes. All coy and little-girly. I can't stand it, makes me feel really old, but sometimes this week it felt like her first dreadful attempts at flirtation too. Did she know what she was doing?

And when we had ice cream cones this afternoon and she offered me hers to taste and then pushed it onto my nose. She laughed so much. I felt then that she was trying to tell me to tiptoe closer. I must have got it wrong. I saw what I wanted to see.

She's nearly at the top of the path now. Maybe she'll stop and put her towel around her. She won't want to walk along Raglan Road in her cozzie. If I put a spurt on, maybe I can catch up with her and talk her round. What shall I say?

I mustn't touch her, that's the most important thing. Even if it would be the most normal thing in the world to catch her up and rub the chill from her darling shoulders with the towel. No, that's the kind of thinking that got me into trouble in the first place. Don't touch her. And don't cry. Swallow it down, the disappointment, the humiliation. You've known worse.

"Mousie! Mummy says won't you stop and wait for her? She's all puffed out. Will you wait for Mummy and we'll have a cream tea at that nice hotel?"

She's slowing down, I think.

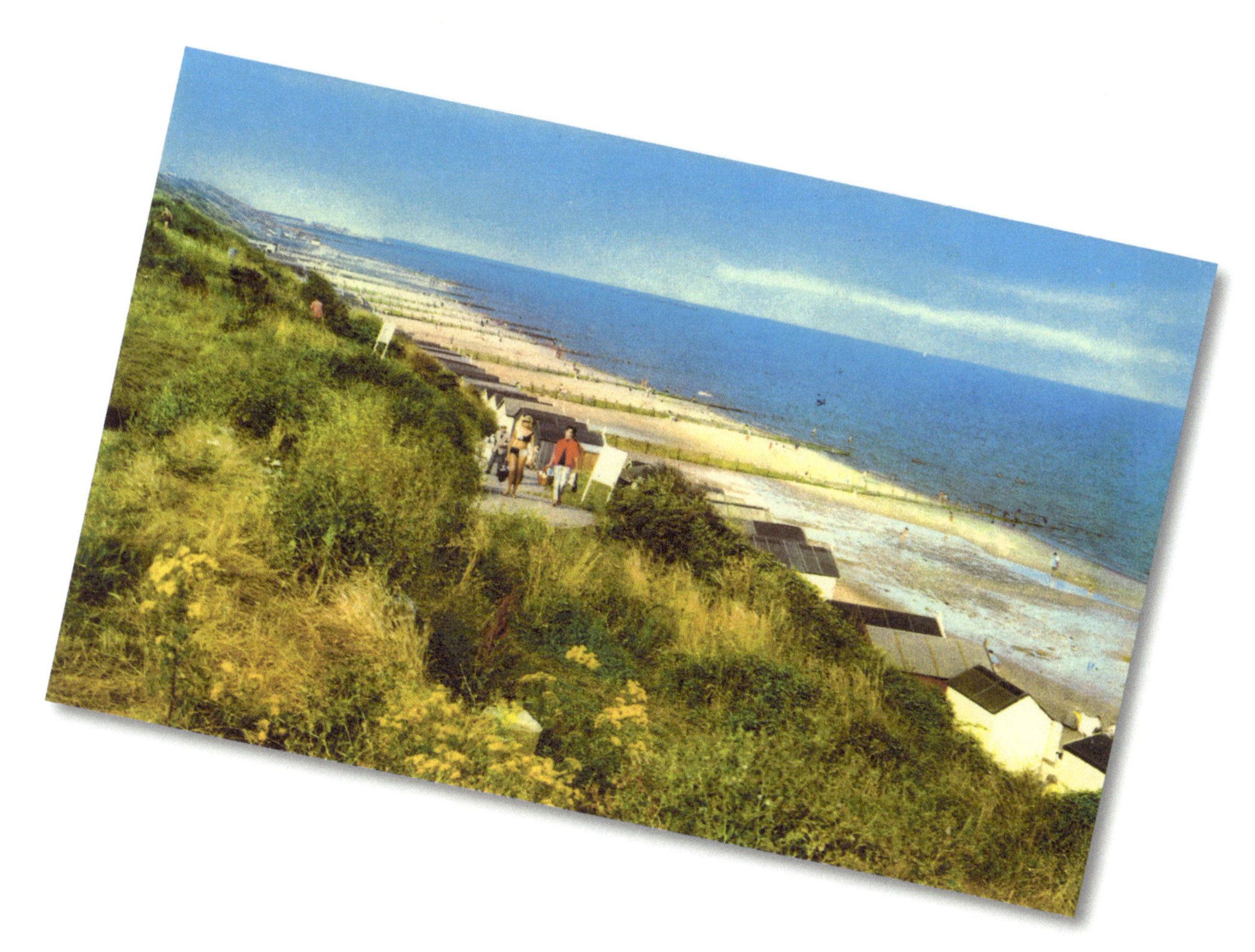

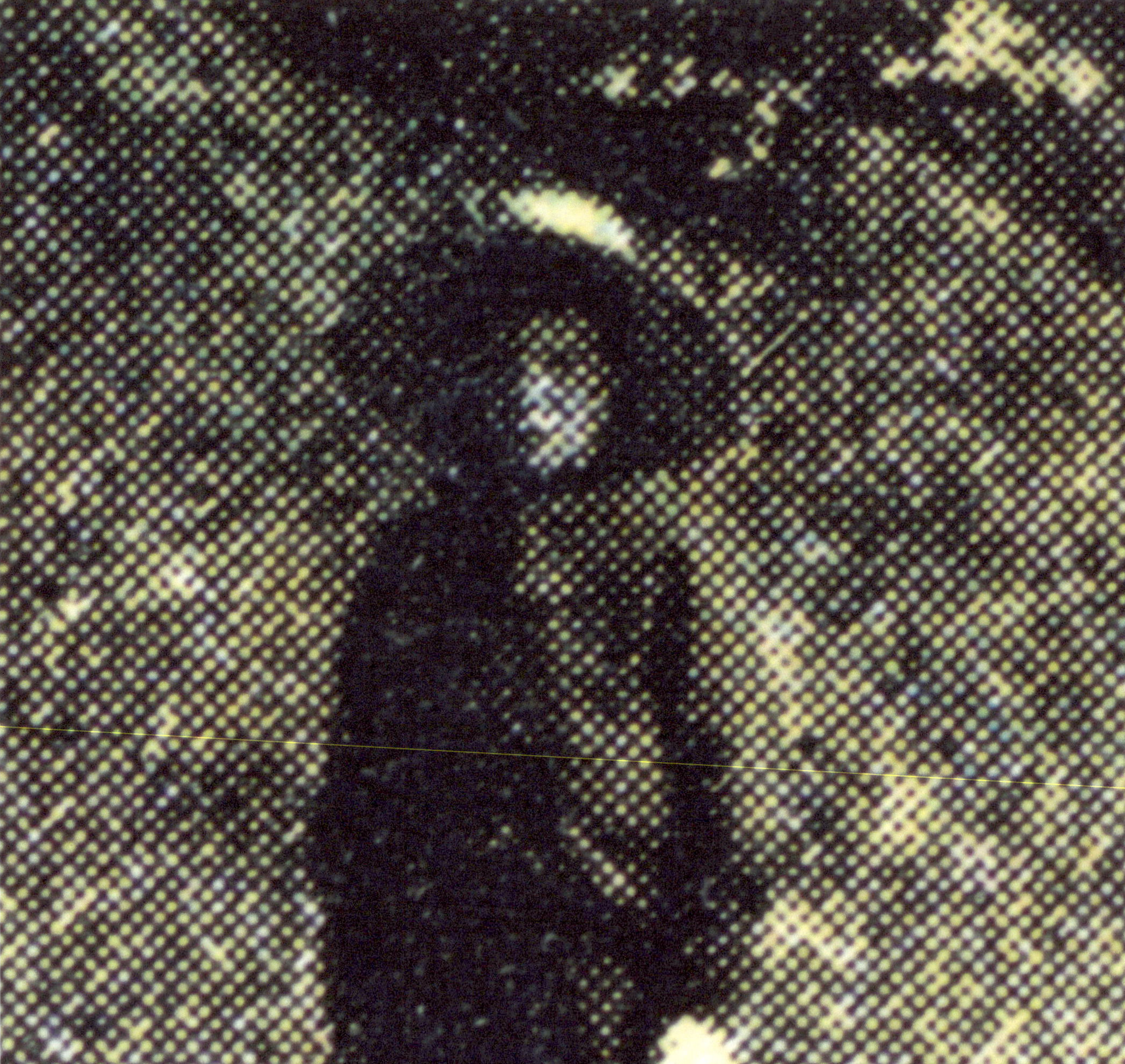

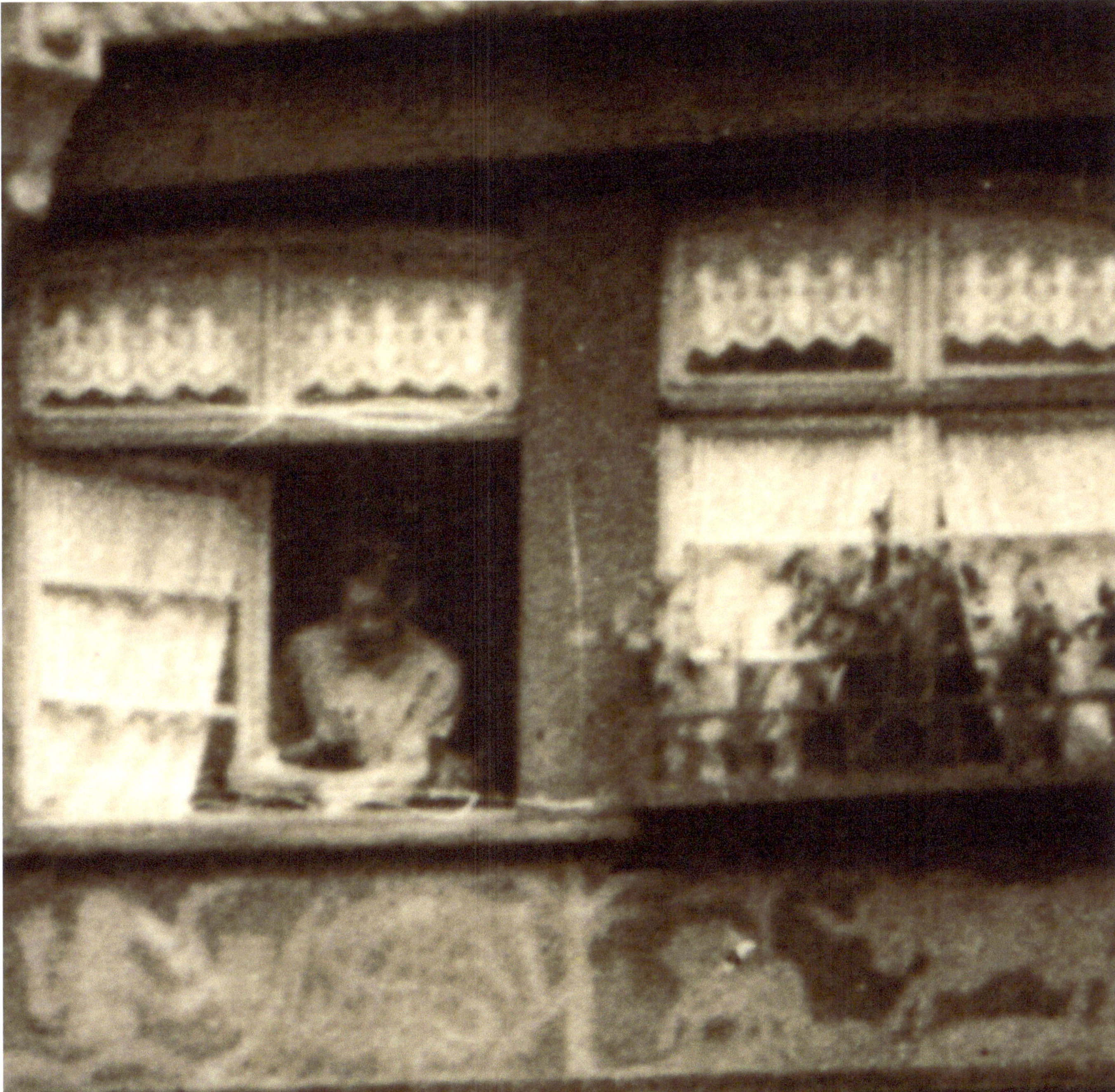

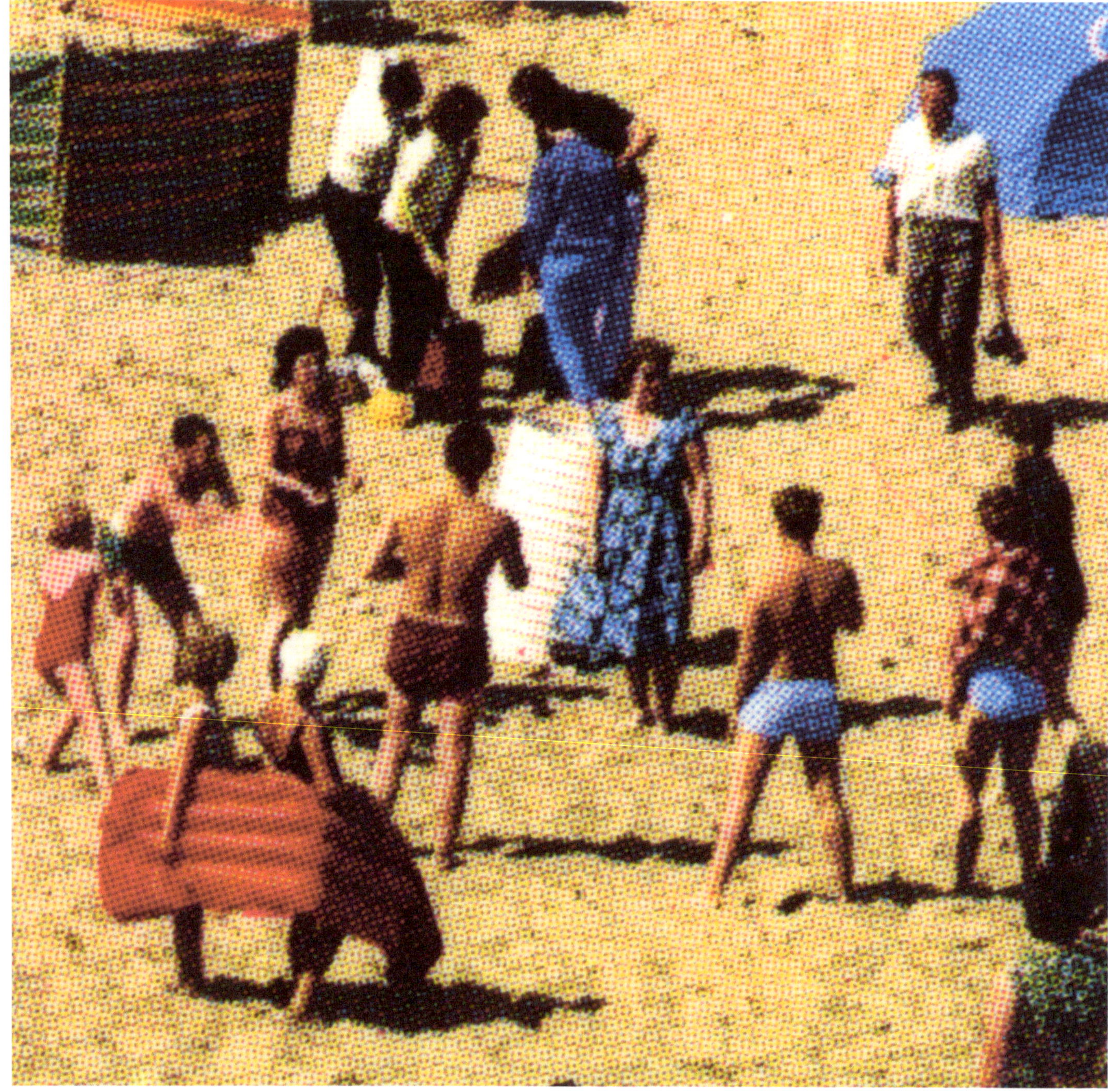

BROADSTAIRS

We came down to Kent very early that Sunday because there was a great deal to be done. We hardly knew where to begin, but we had a map and so we went to the furthest point east, intending to work our way down the coast. At that easternmost point there was a beach called Joss Bay so we made for that, and as we drove down the narrow lane to the clifftop, we saw it stretching away below, calamitously thronged with the denizens of Gomorrah. It was almost impossible to park our van – how is it possible that so many of these people own cars? – and we ended up having to carry all our materials a very long way.

It was a very hot day – I won't make any cheap jibes about Hell because Hell deserves the greatest respect. No doubt the baking sunshine had played a large part in luring these people onto the beach and maddening them into nakedness. The boys felt the heat more than myself and Dymphna as we had the freedom to wear dresses. And they were gallantly carrying almost everything too.

When we got down to the beach we struggled over the sand until we found a little bit of space and we put down the boards and cases. While the boys began to set up our 'chapel', as we like to think of it – just the boards on easels but a sanctuary nonetheless – Dymphna scurried off somewhere. I would need to soon as well. But there was work to be done right away. A group of flagrant sinners stood in a ring just nearby. Nearly naked, laughing – *shrieking* – throwing a ball one to the other to excite themselves. Men and women together in their folly, looking at each other brazenly, delighting in the sight of so much 'strange flesh'. I felt courage flood through my veins and I stepped right into their sinful circle, disrupting their ritual – that was what it seemed to me, their cries so rhythmic and their movements. I wasn't afraid, in any case four of our strong good men were right behind me, should I need aid. But there were four of their men too – all in that disgusting clinging garment such people don at the drop of a hat – "trunks" – flaunting themselves. I couldn't look. I heard one of them guffaw.

There were two women and a girl child as well and I fixed one of the women with my eyes instead. I felt them blaze with zeal, with righteousness.

"Stop! In the name of decency, cover yourselves!"

"Hey, lady, catch!"

Their ball was thrown straight at me, a missile designed to drive me out of their circle. I wasn't about to be deflected from my purpose that easily. I intercepted the ball and flung it back. If I accidentally struck one of the men in his…, well, it would be a victory for good.

"Nice throw!" one of them called out, taunting me. He aimed the ball squarely at me again and it was only thanks to my quick nerves that I was able to catch it and turn it around again. I knew exactly what they were doing: distracting me from my true purpose so that it would be almost impossible for me to show them the error of their ways.

"Satan…" I began.

"She's good! Keep 'em coming, Missus!" yelled the young man directly in front of me, his flesh burnished by the sun like a true savage.

I needed to visit the amenities quite urgently, I now realised. I didn't even know where they were. Which direction had Dymphna headed off in? And where was she? Shouldn't she be back by now? Had she been ensnared by Satan's myrmidons? We've learnt all about their cunning ways in our battle briefings.

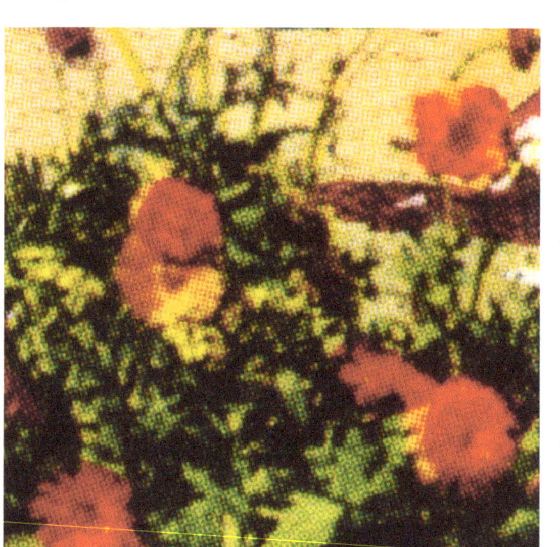

The ball careened towards me again, swerving dangerously, but I parried it and returned fire.

"Yes!" they whooped. "You're a natural!"

"For the sake of that innocent child…" I cried over their increasingly frenzied ululations, "…you must desist from pagan sun worship and… and…"

"Are those lads with you, Missus? Get them over here and we can get a rounders game going. Hey, lads!"

I glanced behind me. Our men were still attending to the easels, which can be very tricky to erect. I didn't think they'd heard. Or, more likely, they were ignoring the worldly blandishments, as we so often have to in our work. Where on earth was Dymphna? I needed her no-nonsense goodness to get to grips with these unrepentants. What would she do? The next time their horrid ball came at me like a bullet, I held on to it. That got their attention.

"Go on, lady, throw it! We were just getting a nice rhythm going." Precisely. It had to be stopped.

"Listen to me. This… this behaviour, this Godless way of life. No good can come of it. On the contrary, only sin…"

"Can we have our ball back, please, Missus?"

They were mocking me, laughing. Now two of them were entangling their limbs in a mock fight, a great brown knot of flesh.

"Believe me, if you don't mend your ways, you'll suffer the vengeance of eternal fire. It's written in…"

"God love her, she's raving mad. What are you on about, 'eternal fire'? We're just having a day on the beach, like everybody else."

It was the tallest of the young men, who stood directly before me and threw his arms out to indicate the thousands of other sinners cavorting

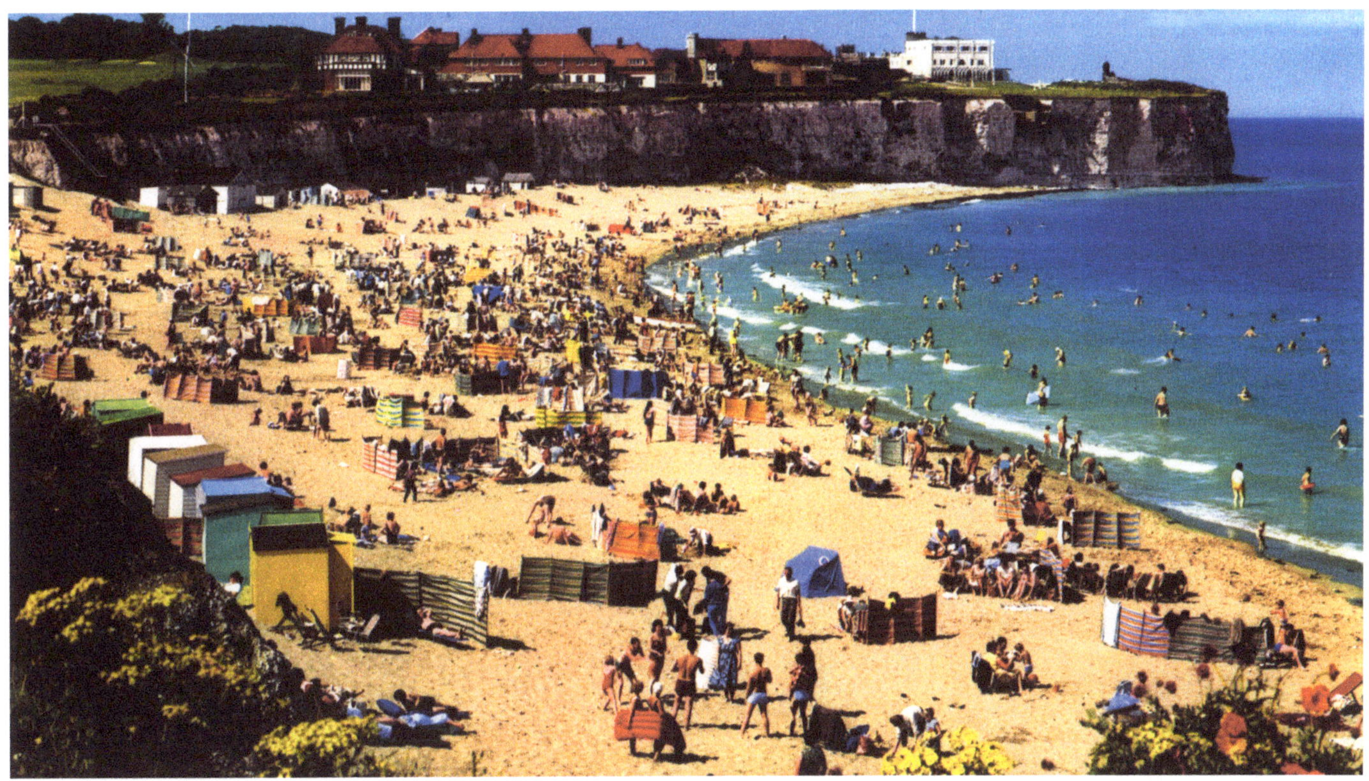

in this second circle of Hell.

"More joy shall be in Heaven over one sinner that repenteth…"

"But, lady, we don't repenteth. We're not bad people, we're just on our holidays."

"Cover your nakedness, be not insolent, the sea of Sodom shall cast up fish, this shall be a sign of the end times…"

"Amanda, get your bucket and spade, I'm not having you hear any more of this filth. Come on, we'll have to move away from these nutters."

They started to pack up their things, towels, deckchairs, picnic basket, shoes. I still had their ball. I held it out to one of the women.

"Listen, love, you can walk away from this, you really can. They've got you in their clutches good and proper, but it's not too late. I've read about these cults, they're really dangerous. One minute they're giving you free soup and the next you're their slave and having their children. We can help you. Do you want to come with us and we'll give you a lift home later? You'll be all right with us, we won't let them harm you. I'm Valerie."

She put her hand on my arm and her brown eyes looked straight into mine. My flesh didn't burn where she touched me. I felt tears threating to flood my eyes.

"I really need to go."

"Yes, you do. You can come with us. You'll be all right."

I couldn't think straight. I turned to the boys. "I'm just, you know… Won't be long."

Valerie squeezed my arm and smiled. "That's it. Well done. We'll go without making a fuss. Come on, Mandy, love."

We set off together across the burning sand.

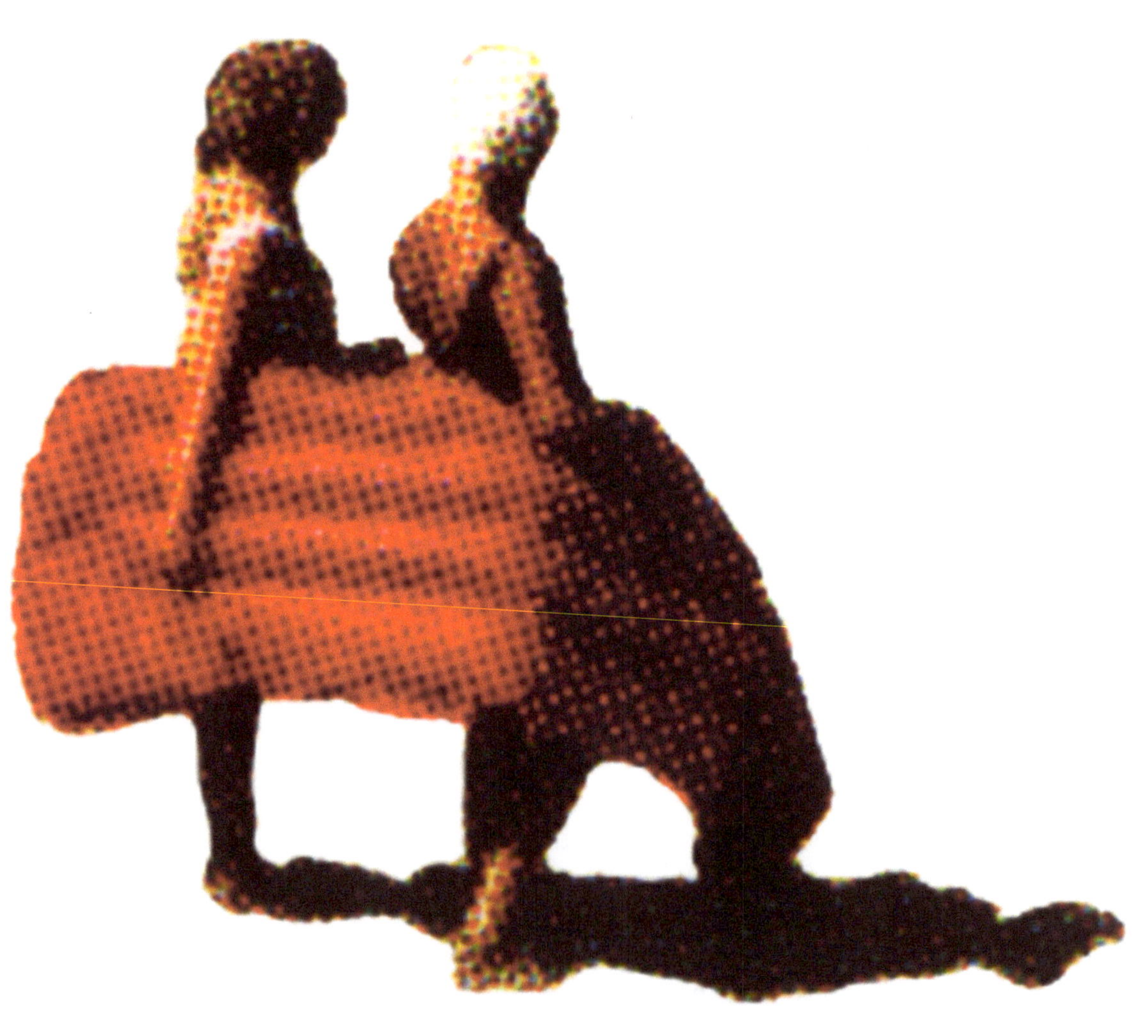

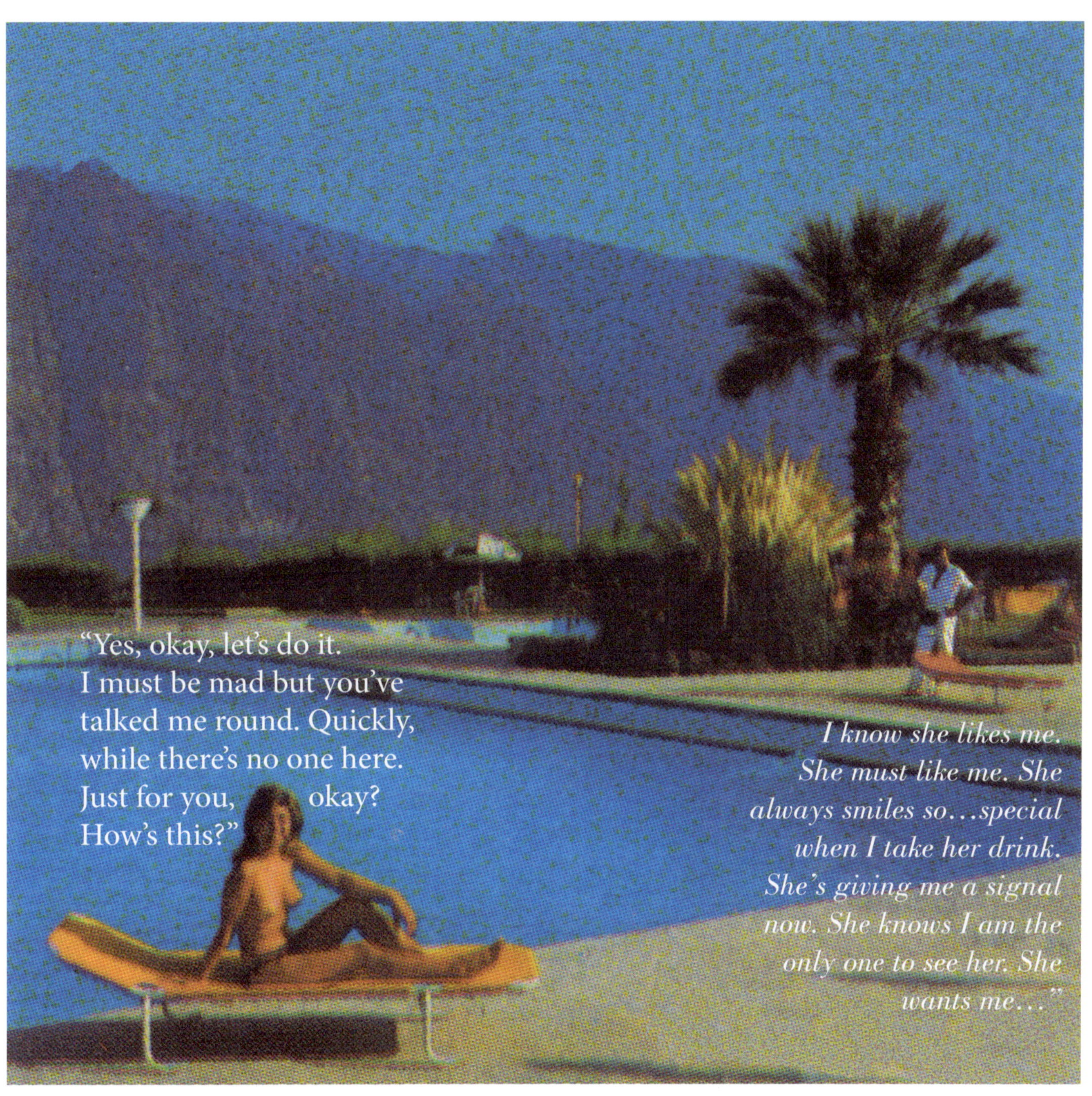
"Yes, okay, let's do it.
I must be mad but you've
talked me round. Quickly,
while there's no one here.
Just for you,   okay?
How's this?"

I know she likes me.
She must like me. She
always smiles so…special
when I take her drink.
She's giving me a signal
now. She knows I am the
only one to see her. She
wants me…"

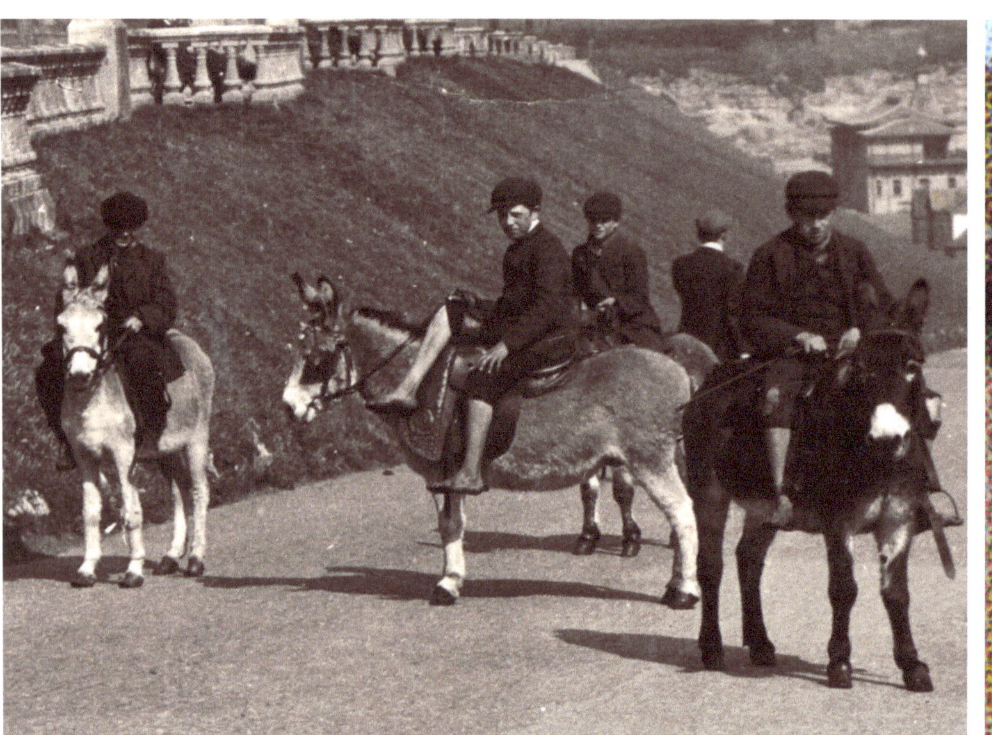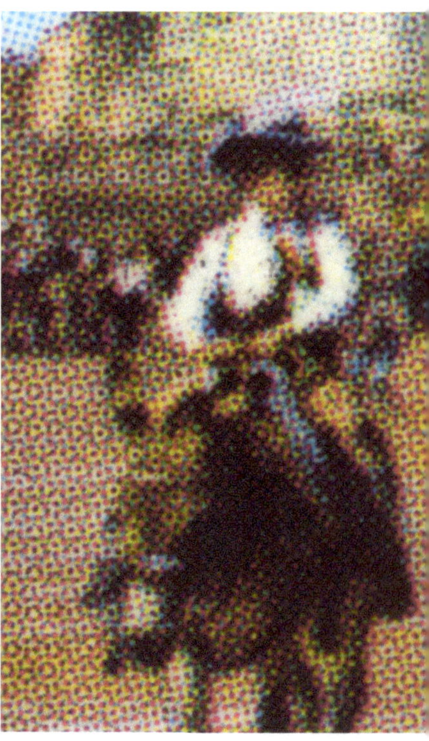

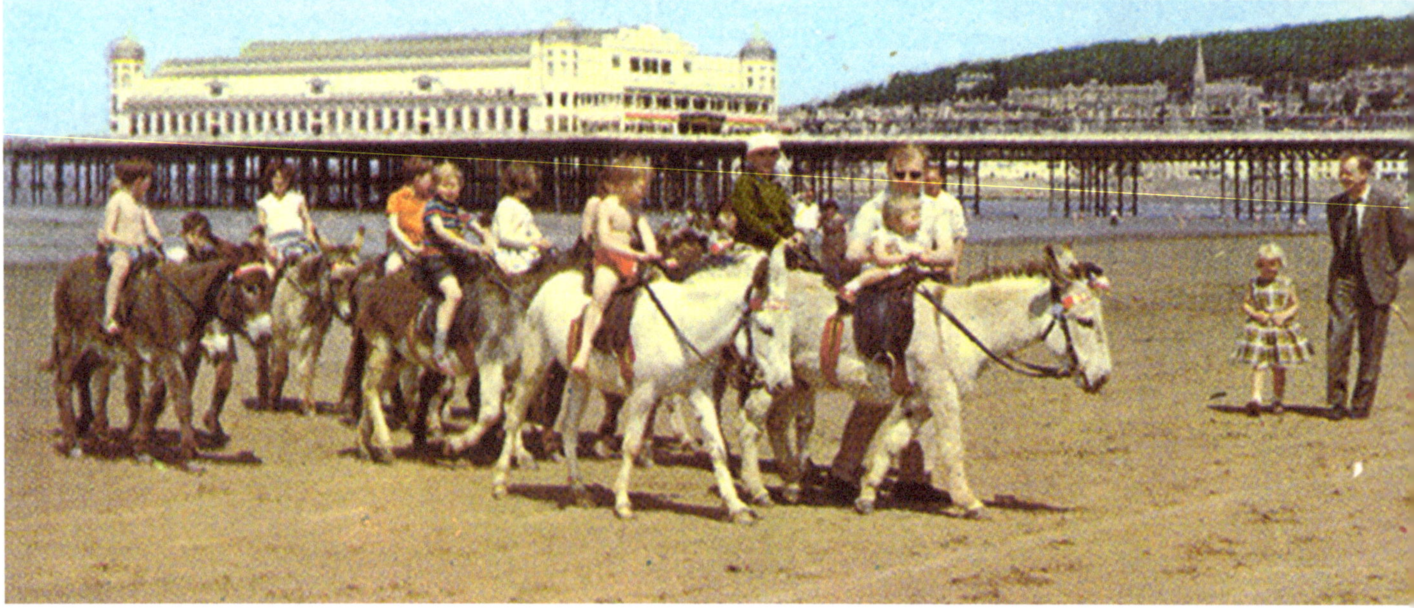

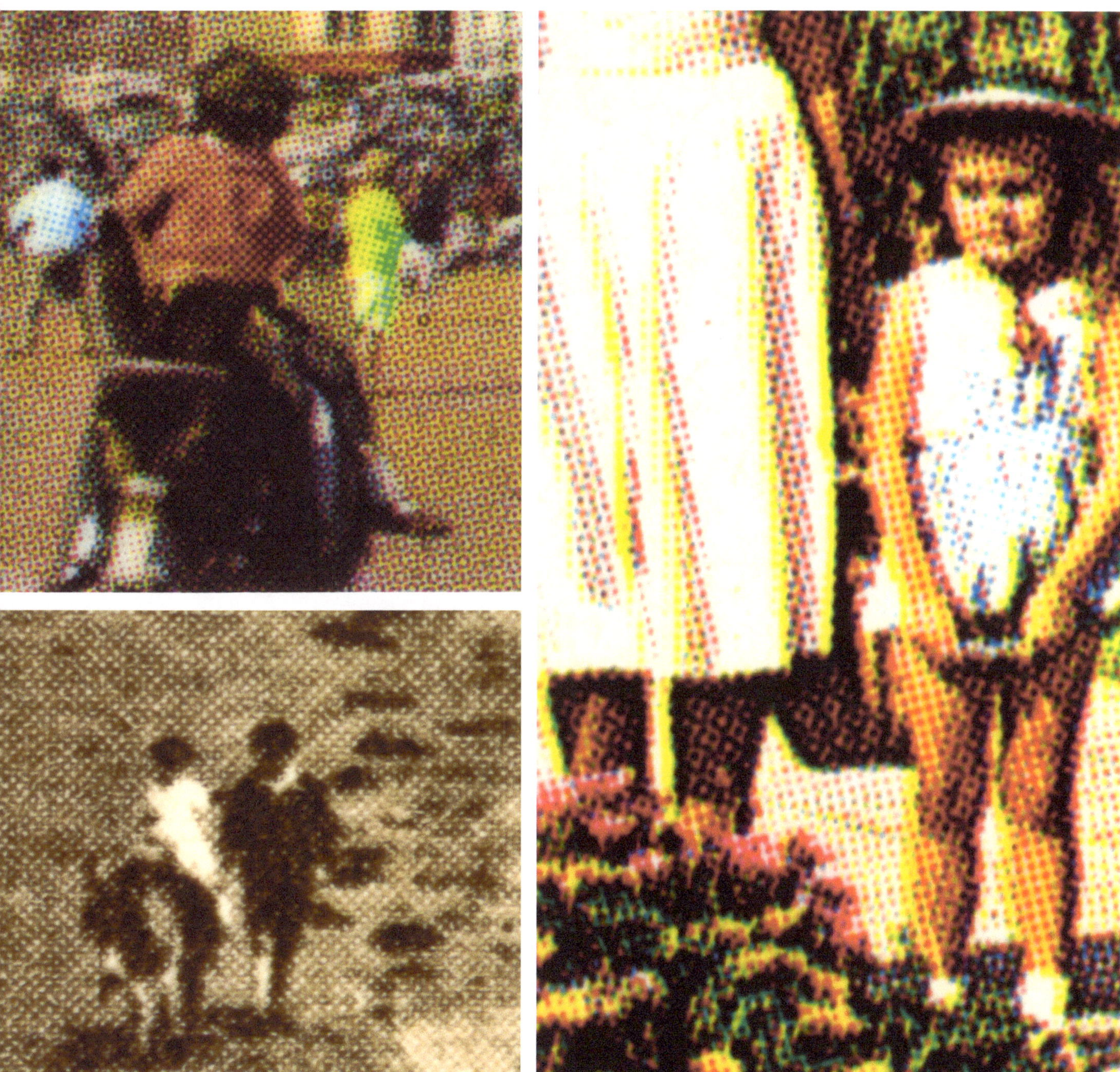

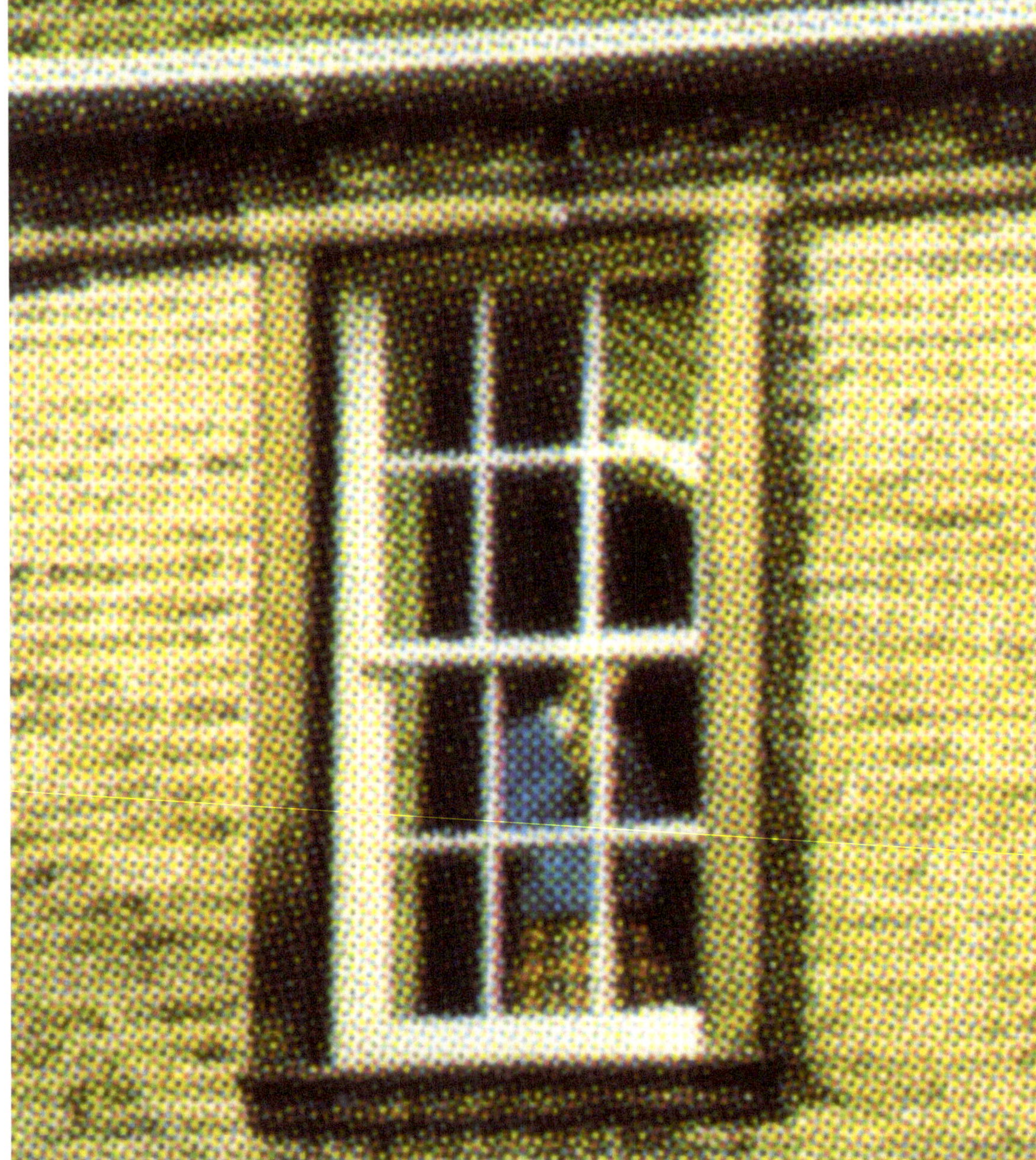

BRONTE PARSONAGE

"Ah, thank you, Linda – I mean, Tabby – yes, show everyone in, please. Come in, ah come in! Well, actually I'm not going to attempt the accent, it would only be an embarrassment – begorrah! – you see what I mean. But I've donned an Irish kilt today in honour of Mr Patrick Bronte, yes, I've gone the extra mile, as we're marking the centenary of his death with this special event.

"Well, let's get everyone into the room first. Can some of you move around to the other side of the bed? In you come, my goodness, what a lot of you. Squeeze in! Don't trip over the trunk. Oh dear, have you snagged your stockings? Yes, that's the trunk he brought over from Ireland with him.

"Can everyone hear me? So, here we are in Mr Bronte's bedroom, Mr Patrick Bronte, the father of our marvellous trio of writers, Charlotte, Emily and Anne – and of course of Branwell Bronte, his only son. We'll come on to him in a moment. As you'll have gathered, Patrick Bronte was Irish, he was born in County Down in 1777, the eldest of ten children. And the family's name was the much more Irish-sounding Brunty – they were humble folk, Patrick's father was a farmhand. Patrick himself was apprenticed to a blacksmith and then perhaps that didn't work out as he was later apprenticed to a linen weaver. However, by the age of sixteen he was in charge of the village school. A bright lad, clearly, and this had been spotted, thankfully.

"By some sort of miracle, or, more likely, a great deal of study and some help from local priests, he won a place at St John's College in Cambridge in 1802. And it was there that he altered the spelling of his surname to the rather distinguished version borne by his daughters. Some have speculated that he made a play on the similarity of his name to the Greek word for 'thunder', which is rather fab, is it not?

"Now, as a young man without any family money, there weren't too many options open to him, and so it was that he was ordained as a minister, in 1807 that would be, and began a whole series of postings around the country as a curate – in Essex, Shropshire and then, hurrah, in our own Yorkshire. He had turned his back on Ireland for good by now. In the course of establishing himself, he had met his wife, Maria Branwell, and they wed in Guiseley in 1812. It wasn't until 1820 that Mr Bronte was given the curateship of Haworth, Stanbury and Oxenhope and the family moved into this house. This was a perpetual role, so he had tenure for life and could really think about putting down roots for the first time. At that point there were six children, including their two eldest, Maria and Elizabeth. But then the family tragedies began.

"Poor Maria, his wife, succumbed to cancer just one year later, in 1821, leaving all those little ones motherless. Her sister Elizabeth mercifully moved up from Cornwall to look after them and 'Aunt Branwell' became the closest thing they had to a mother. This bedroom that we're standing in now was the room that Patrick moved into after his wife died – before that they had the room just across the landing, yes, the room you were in just before. He certainly never seemed to entertain any thoughts of remarrying.

"Now, there are guides waiting in each room to tell you about other aspects of the family's history. So I must stick to just my part of the story. Mr Bronte spent a great deal of time in this room as he famously went up to bed at nine o'clock each night, always saying to his grown-up children, who would be gathered in the dining room downstairs, not to be too late to bed. He would wind the clock on the landing, then it was up to this room.

"When his son Branwell descended into opium and alcohol addiction, Mr Bronte had him share this room so that he could keep a close eye on him. There was a fear that he might smoke in bed and set the place on fire, it seems. Branwell died at the age of thirty-one, in here perhaps. I'm not absolutely sure – we can ask the curator later, if it's of interest.

"Now, here we come to the special part of today – for me, at all events. They were rough old times they lived in, in the first half of the nineteenth century. There was a lot of anti-clerical feeling, you had your Luddites and your Chartists in big numbers in the area, neither of them great fans of priests. Mr Bronte took to keeping a loaded pistol by his bed at night, just in case there was any trouble. Can I just reach into that drawer, madam? Sorry to trouble you, we're rather packed in, aren't we?

"Yes, this is a pistol of the period. Not the actual pistol, but of the type. No need to worry! I can hear one or two murmurs of alarm. I've been shown how to use it properly.

"Mr Bronte lived until the age of eighty-four, his eyesight deteriorating pretty badly. He died on June seventh, 1861, exactly one hundred years ago today, and that of course is the reason we're having this special enactment day, to mark the centenary. I've been given permission to re-enact this particular habit of Mr Bronte's in celebration of his life and the life he made here for his wonderful daughters.

"He was nothing if not a man of habit, Mr Bronte, and every morning he would discharge the bullet that he had loaded into his pistol the night before by – yes, I just need to lift up the sash window here, oof, bit stiff… – by firing it out of the window and across the churchyard.

"Like this. Good gracious! What a bang! Oh dear, there's some fellow down there with a camera and tripod. I've put the fear of God into him, by the looks of it. Don't worry, sir, it's only a blank! Oh dear, he's running off… Ah, well, that's the end of my bit, ladies and gentlemen. If you'd like to make your way into Branwell's studio, which is just next door, Mr Lazenby will tell you a little more about that unfortunate young man. I know he's dressed the part, not sure if he'll have had a tipple…

"Now, I'd better go down and see if I can find that photographer…"

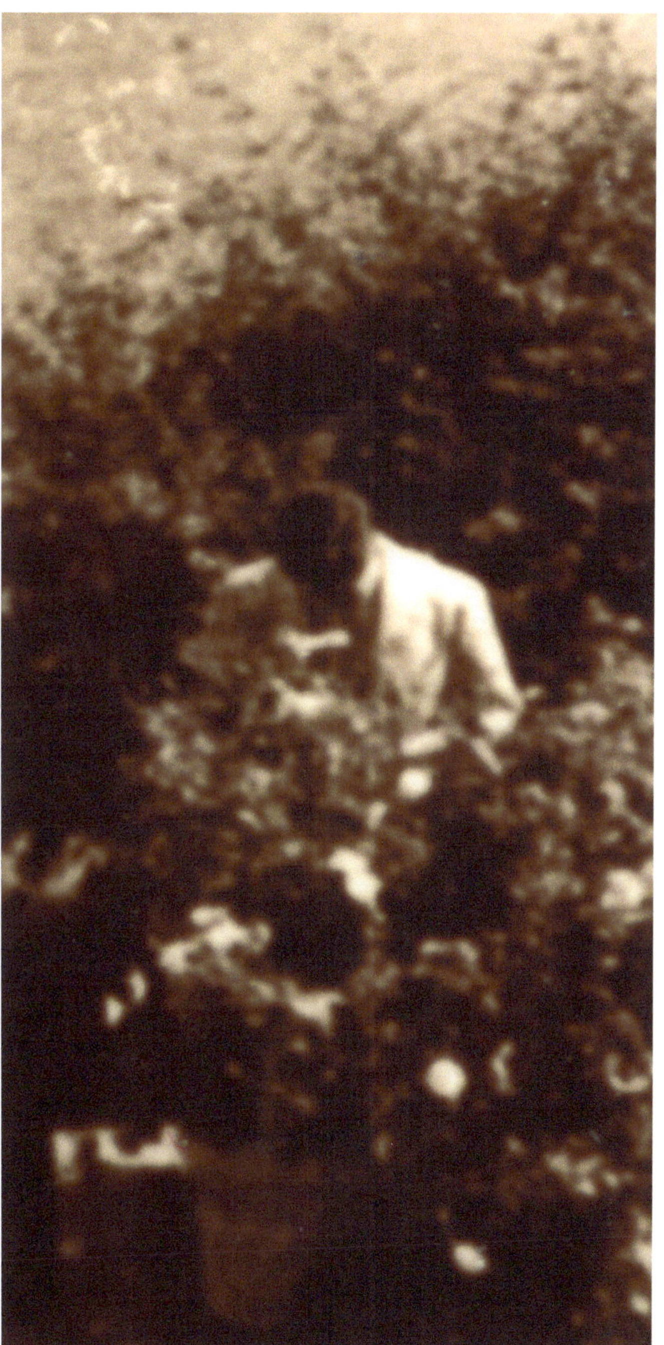

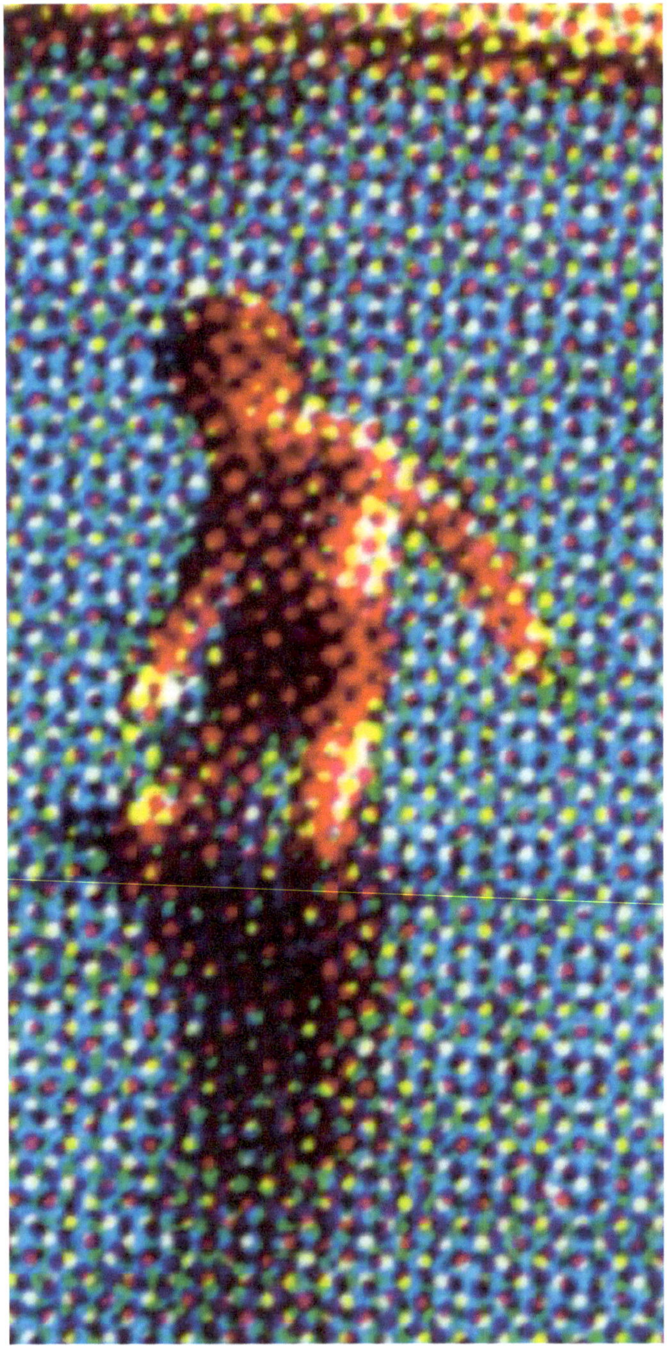

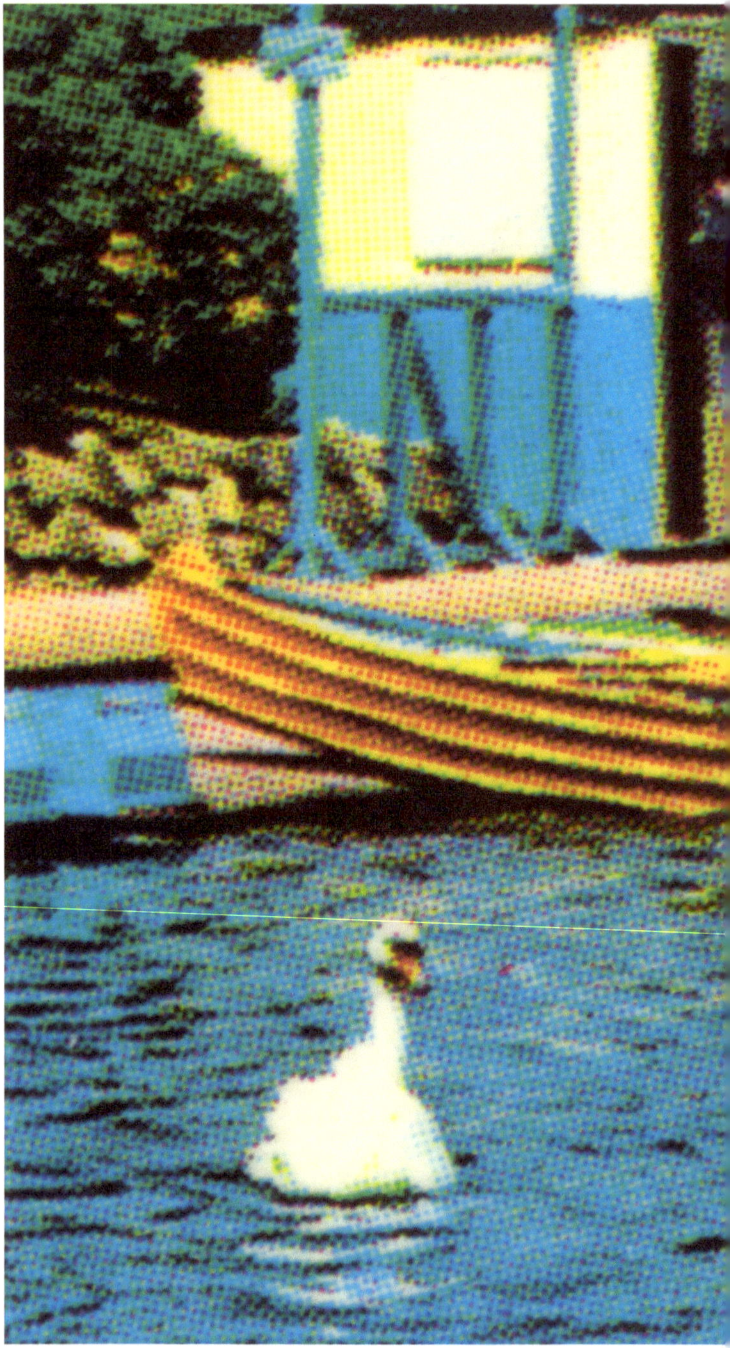

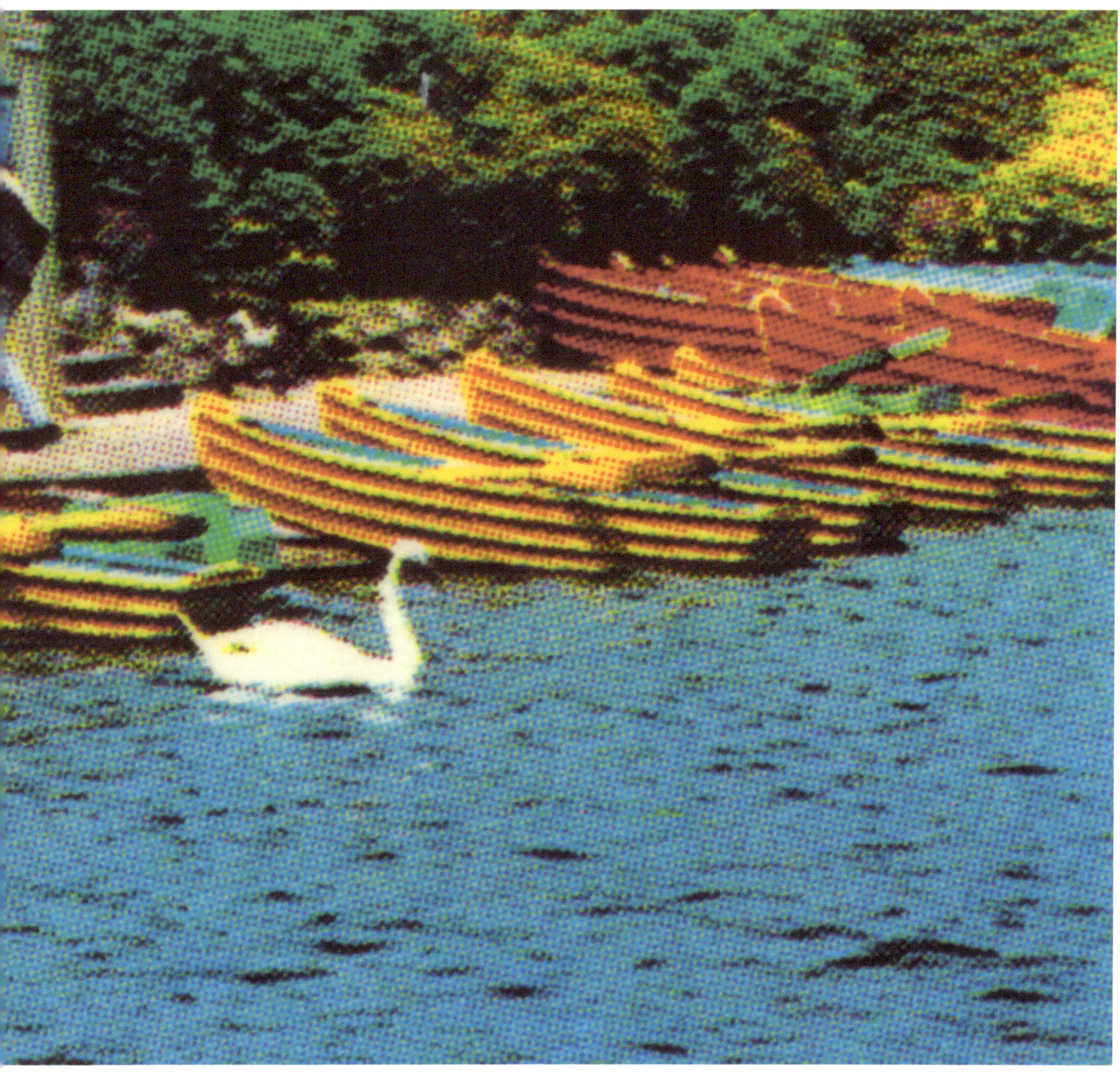

BIDEFORD

I named the boys. They were my problem and I wasn't going to have any Tobiases or Donovans or whatever nonsense the girls wanted. John and Simon. You can't go wrong if you stick to the disciples. If there had been female disciples I would have chosen those for the girls too. The fashion was all for Victoriana when they were born and I may have been swayed. I was younger then and things seemed easier. Were easier.

You'd think the boys were twins, just like Marion and Vanessa, not cousins. Oh but I always forget (just for a blessed moment) that they are half-brothers too, or so I firmly believe. Em and Vee seem to know whose is whose, which is just as well, I suppose, not that it makes much difference. It's hard to remember, now, what it was like when they were at St Cedric's: the lovely peace during term time, G and Ts before supper, quiet weekends on the boat. And to think that Vanessa was curious about the art world and Marion talked of working in a bank. I remember I asked Mrs Greave to talk to Vee about her little gallery and I could have got Mr Parsons to start Em in our branch, I'm sure. What a stifling disappointment it all is.

If the girls would just tell me what happened, I could sue that school. I could close it down. There would be some small satisfaction in that. I feel absolutely certain a master was involved. My money's on that art teacher. The blond hair's the giveaway. I spoke to him once or twice, a ridiculous man, all that Brideshead nonsense, the teddy bear! He seemed to live in tennis whites, though it hardly seemed practical for an art master. I've racked my brains to see whether I can remember the girls ever talking about him, if they had a crush on him, if they ever mentioned him organising some inappropriate event in the evenings. Nothing. And I can get nothing whatsoever out of the girls about it now.

I'll never forget that day when the school rang and said could we collect them as they were both expecting. That was the day my life ended. It plays in my head again and again, there's no relief from the shame. The two of them, become stout, already obviously 'with child', standing in the headmistress's office with seemingly no sense of shame on their part. I wonder, now, whether they even understood what was happening to them. Apparently, it was the other girls who began to tittle-tattle when they saw them in the showers each morning, until it reached the ears of the staff. And of course since everyone knew about it, there was no question of any sort of discreet solution, no, we were well and truly stuck with the situation.

One of my girls expecting would have been a calamity, but for both of them to have been impregnated – it seems simultaneously – was beyond comprehension. What fiend did this

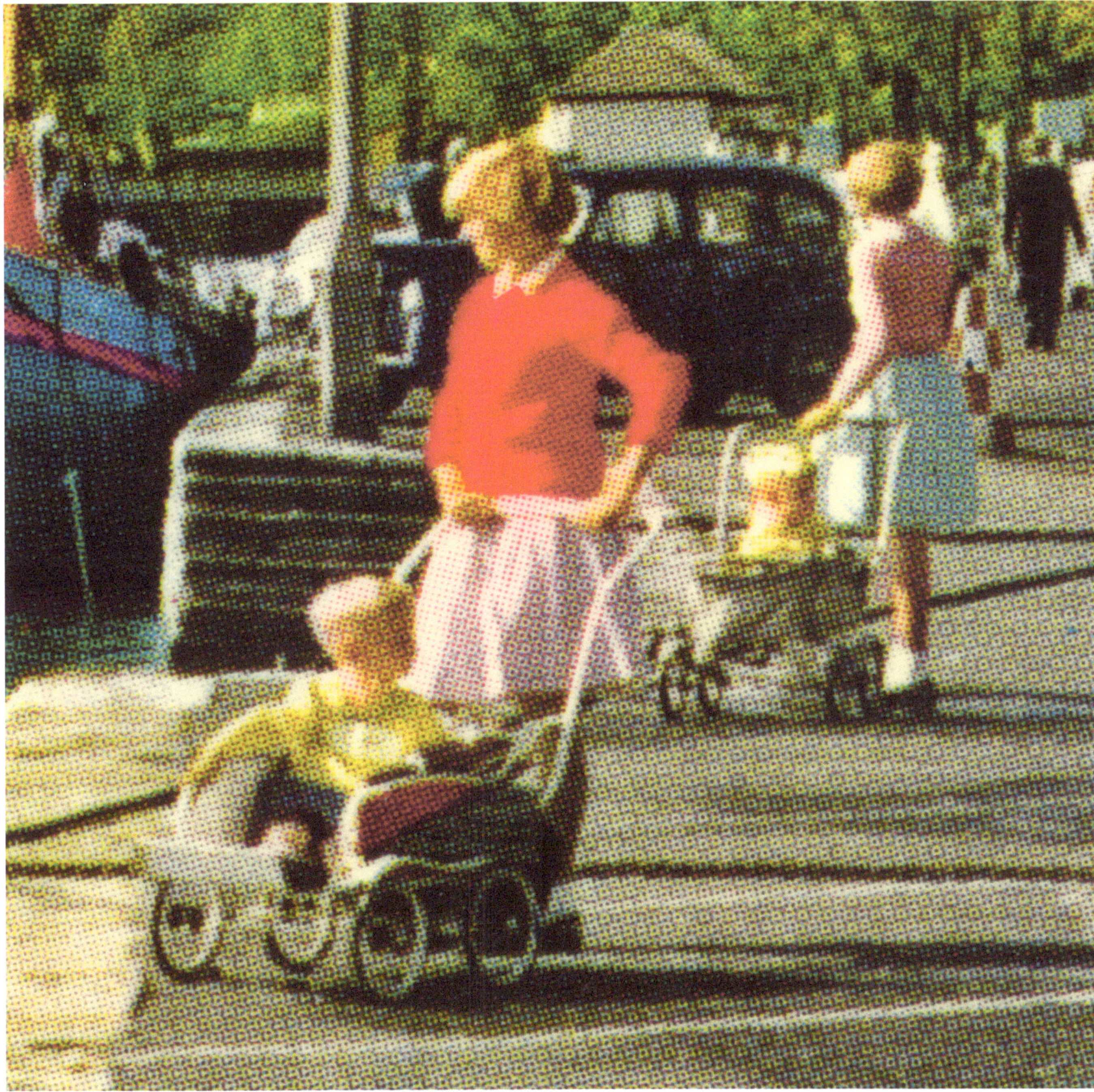

to them – to me? Why won't they tell me? Not knowing is killing me. Well, now Vanessa and Marion can look after their brats the way I looked after them, giving up my lovely job at Top Dog, not to mention my figure, and my freedom. I will dress them and feed them and give them a roof over their heads – them and their little blond bastards – but let them never forget for one second that they behaved like half-witted children and got themselves into this state. Did that school teach them nothing about biology?

They don't like the outfits I choose for them. *Boo hoo*. When they earn their own money they can dress as they please. For now, the choice is mine. I've heard them muttering to each other in that secret language they've had since they were tiny. No doubt whining about me and my 'meanness'. When I hear them whispering their *iggybiggyboos*, it's like a switch being thrown. I elbow my way in between them and send them skittering apart. That puts a stop to it for a while.

See them now with those ugly 'strollers' (much cheaper than a Silver Cross pram though). Marion is gazing at the boats, perhaps she's remembering the happy times she had on our lovely little skiff. Well, the skiff had to be sold to pay for the strollers and everything else. As for Vanessa, *quelle surprise*, she's looking at a man. Has she still not learned her lesson?

Well, if there's a man in all of England prepared to take them off my hands, he's welcome to them, but I shan't waste my time in feverish hope. He'd have to take both of them as they're inseparable. No doubt that played a part in their downfall. Ugh, I can't bear to think of it.

"Jeremy! *Jeremy!* Don't dawdle so. We'll sit on the benches along here and have our sandwiches. John and Simon can toddle about. Yes, the girls will have to keep a close eye on them. I said it wasn't very safe last time we came, if you recall, but at least it's nice and quiet."

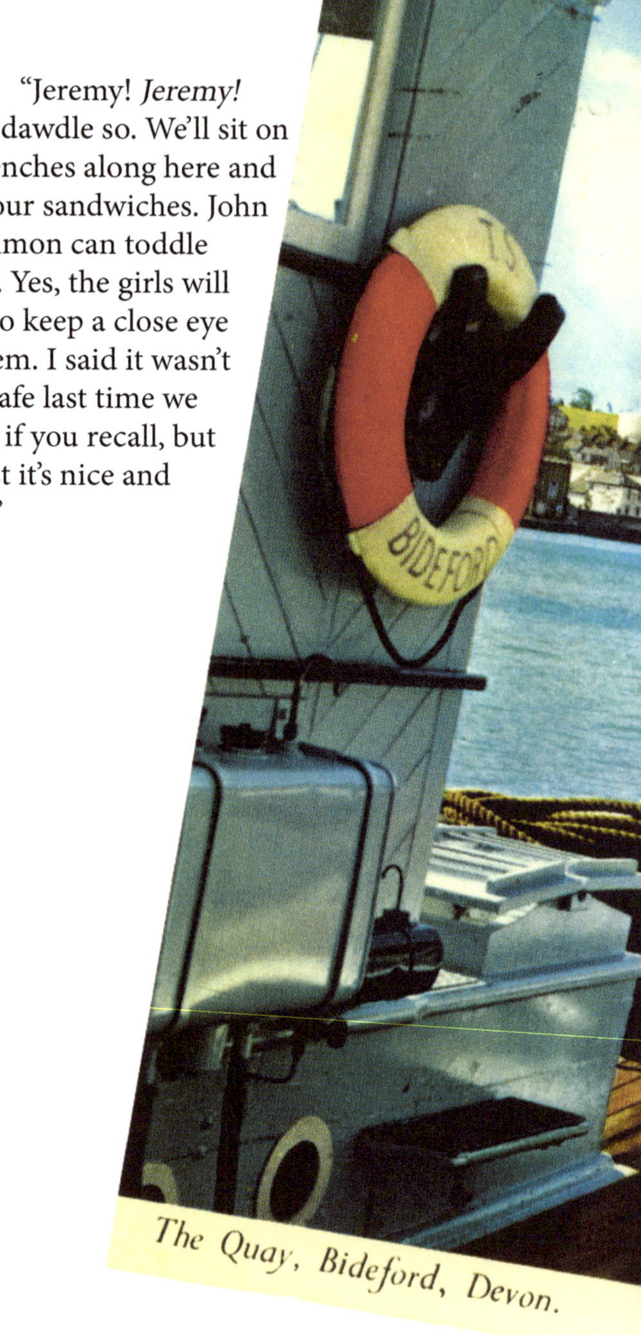

The Quay, Bideford, Devon.

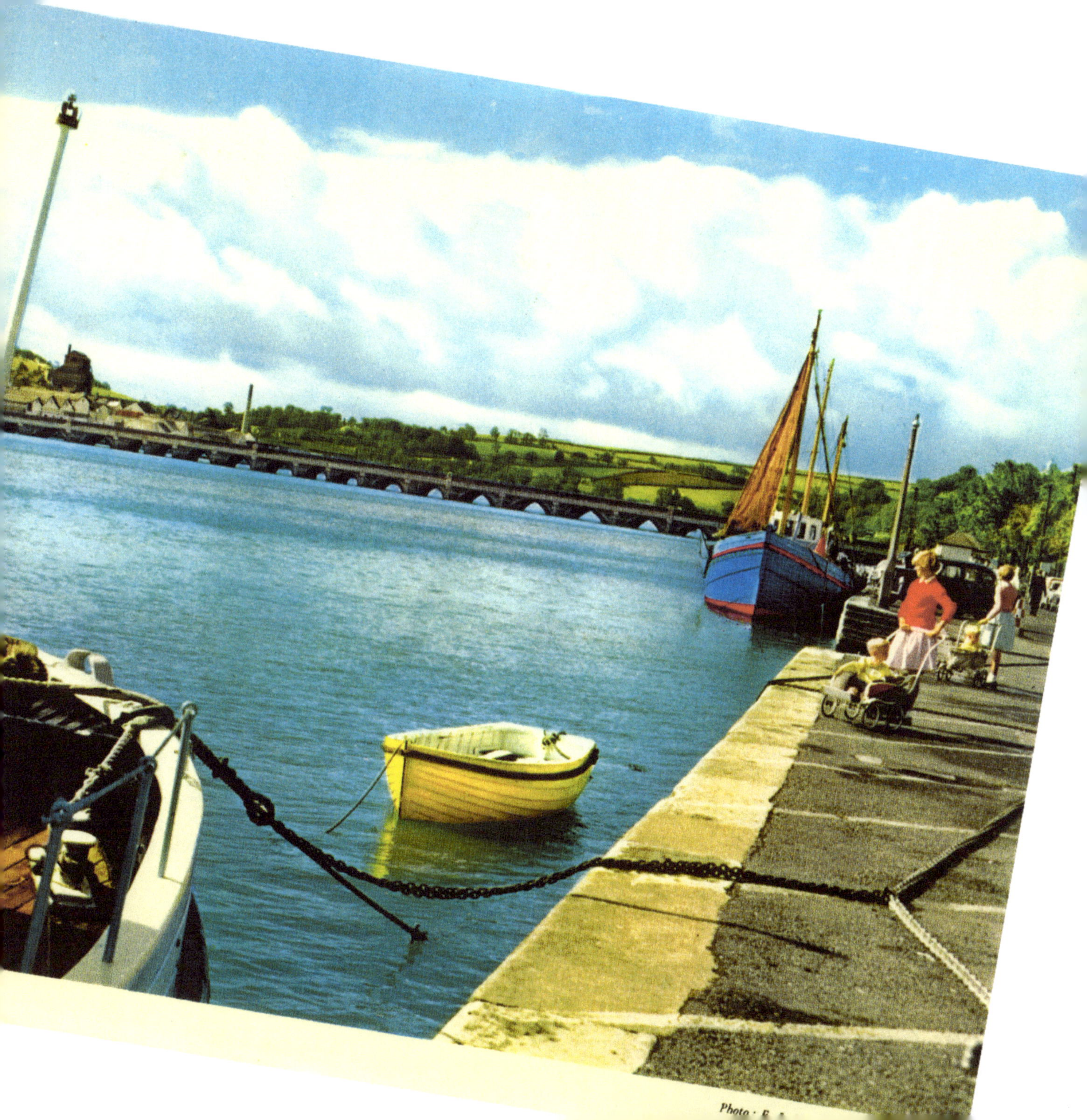

Photo · F

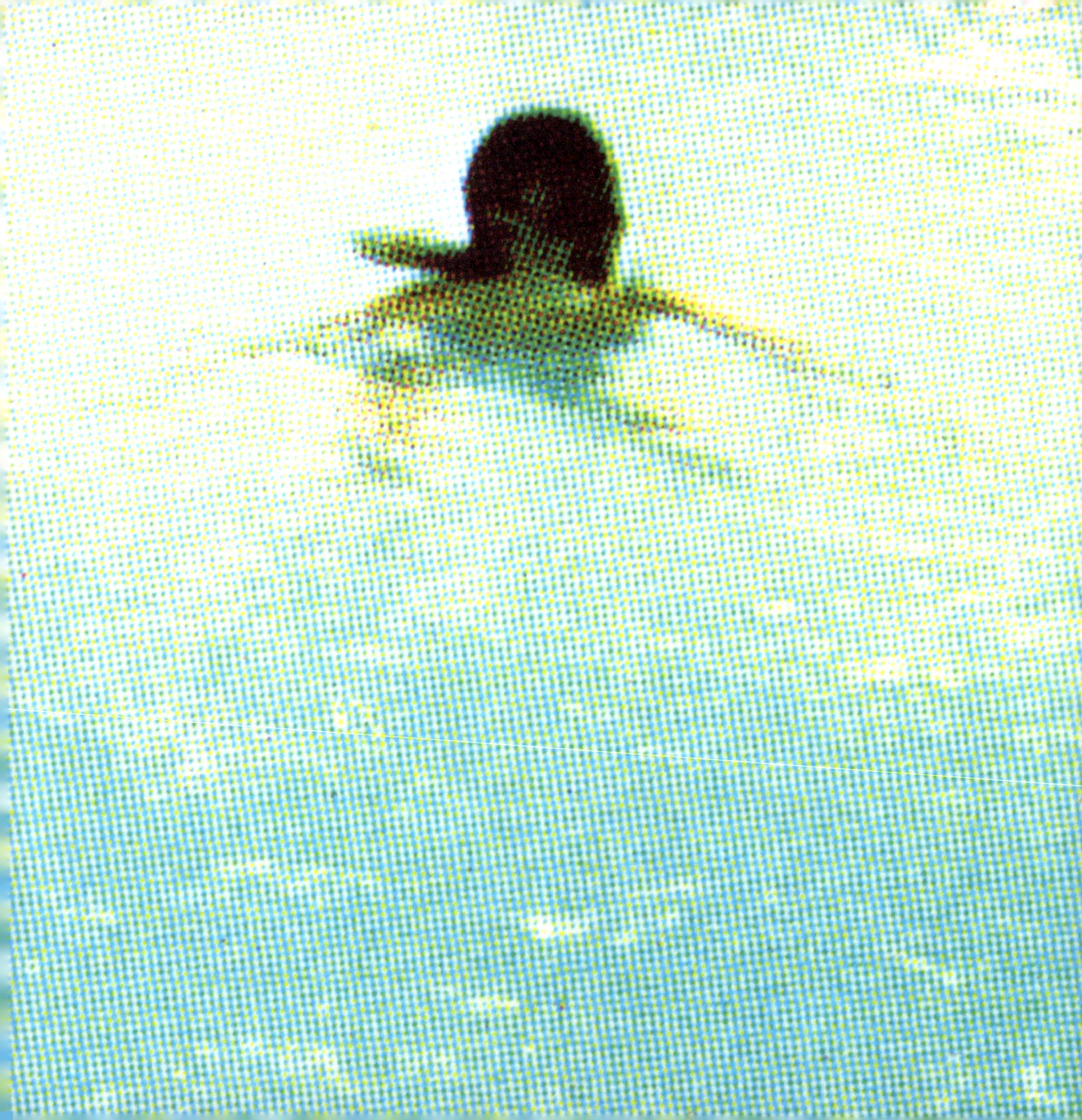

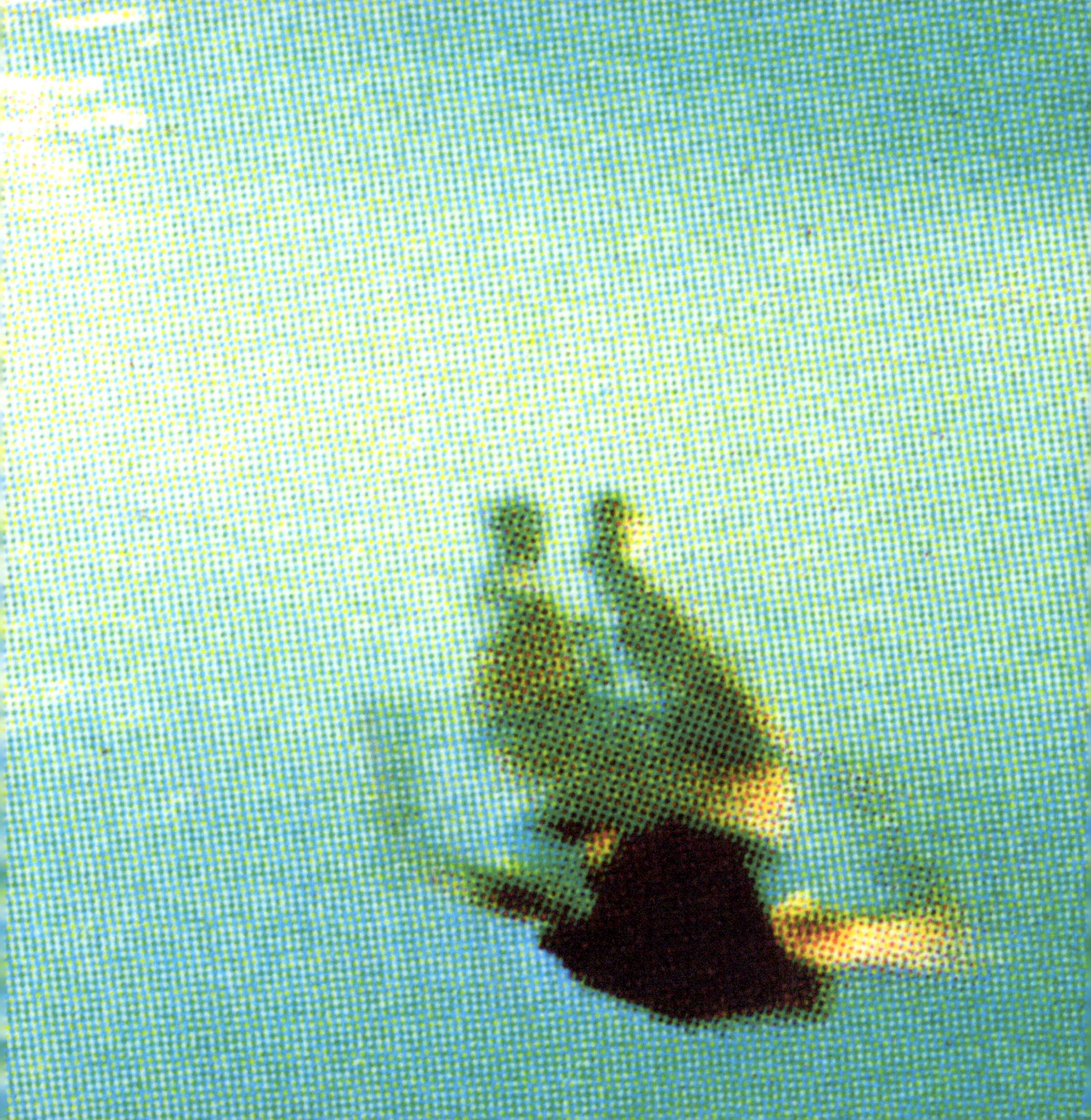

DERBY

"She's been gone ages."

"She said not to budge."

"I'm dead bored."

"She'll kill us if we're not right here when she comes out."

"We could just go inside the doors a little bit, to see if she's coming?"

"No, she won't like it. Anyway, I've been in before, on our school trip."

"Not much of a school trip, that."

"It weren't our main school trip. That were to the Heights of Abraham. There's a suit of armour in there we could look at."

"At the Heights of Abraham?"

"No, you idiot, in there, in the Council House."

"We live in a council house, don't we, but it dun't look much like that."

"It's different, in't it? You see that little table, over there, on the roundabout? That's a fountain. I've seen it when it's on."

"Just think if you were having your tea at that table and all of a sudden water started shooting out."

"It's not a real table, it just looks like one. Where's Mam, anyway? I'm fed up waiting."

"Maybe she's gone in to pay the rent? She goes there for that."

"No, that's Thursdays she does that and today's Tuesday. I know, maybe she went in to complain about that rat we saw in our yard. They do 'pest control' in there – they told us about it on our visit. This man came out of his room in really big wellies and said he was the Ratcatcher."

"Maybe he'll be round our yard soon then."

"I'm cold. I wish I had my cardy."

"Me too. We could just move by the door, out of the wind."

"We could, but you know what she's like. She'll yell if we've moved an inch when she comes out. She can't be much longer cos she's been in there ages."

"Look at all them people waiting for the bus. Lucy Salmon's up there with her Mam. I hope our Mam doesn't yell at us cos they'll all hear. I hate Lucy Salmon."

"She should only be allowed out at Christmas, like the tin of salmon Mam always keeps for our tea on Boxing Day."

"I bet she stinks like it did last year when Mam opened the tin. It must go off, it's that old."

"No, it never goes off. That's why you've got to have tins in the cupboard if there's a nuclear war. Don't you remember that film they showed us in assembly?"

"I wasn't listening. It was too scary."

"I tell you what's scary. I saw Uncle Dave going in there before."

"You never said."

"Well, I know you don't like him. He just ran up the steps and in, like a rat up a drainpipe."

"Maybe the Ratcatcher'll get him, then."

"He's not our uncle. I won't call him that any more. I'll just call him Dave. He can lump it if he doesn't like it. What's he want in there, any road?"

"Dunno. I hate it when Mam gives him his tea at our house."

"And the rest."

"What's the rest?"

"You're too little to know."

"I am not."

"Yes you are. Oh, here she comes now."

"He's with her."

"She's holding his hand."

"Shh, she'll hear."

"June, Sandra, this is your new Dad! We just got married, in there. What a laugh! Now why are the pair of you looking like a wet Wednesday? I know you missed out but Dave's only got his lunch hour so there was no messing about. Come on, I'll take you to Bennett's cafe for a treat. You can have salmon sandwiches if you like, seeing as it's a special occasion."

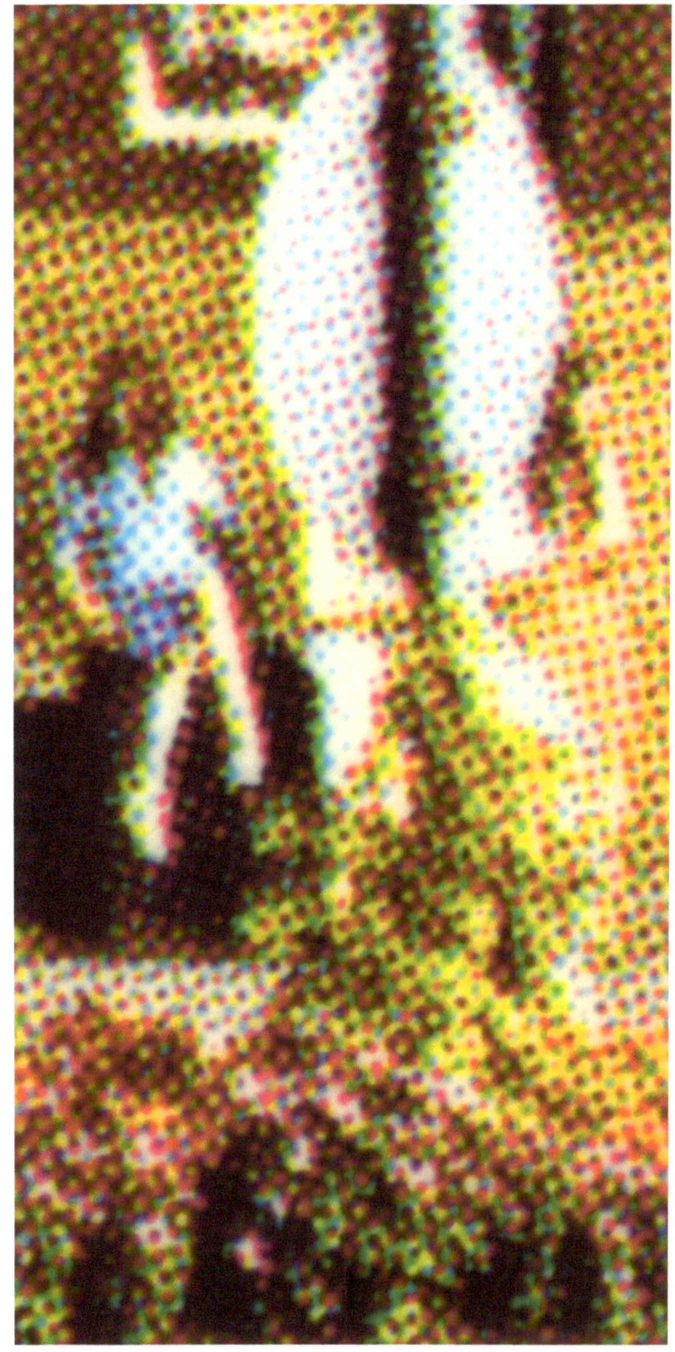

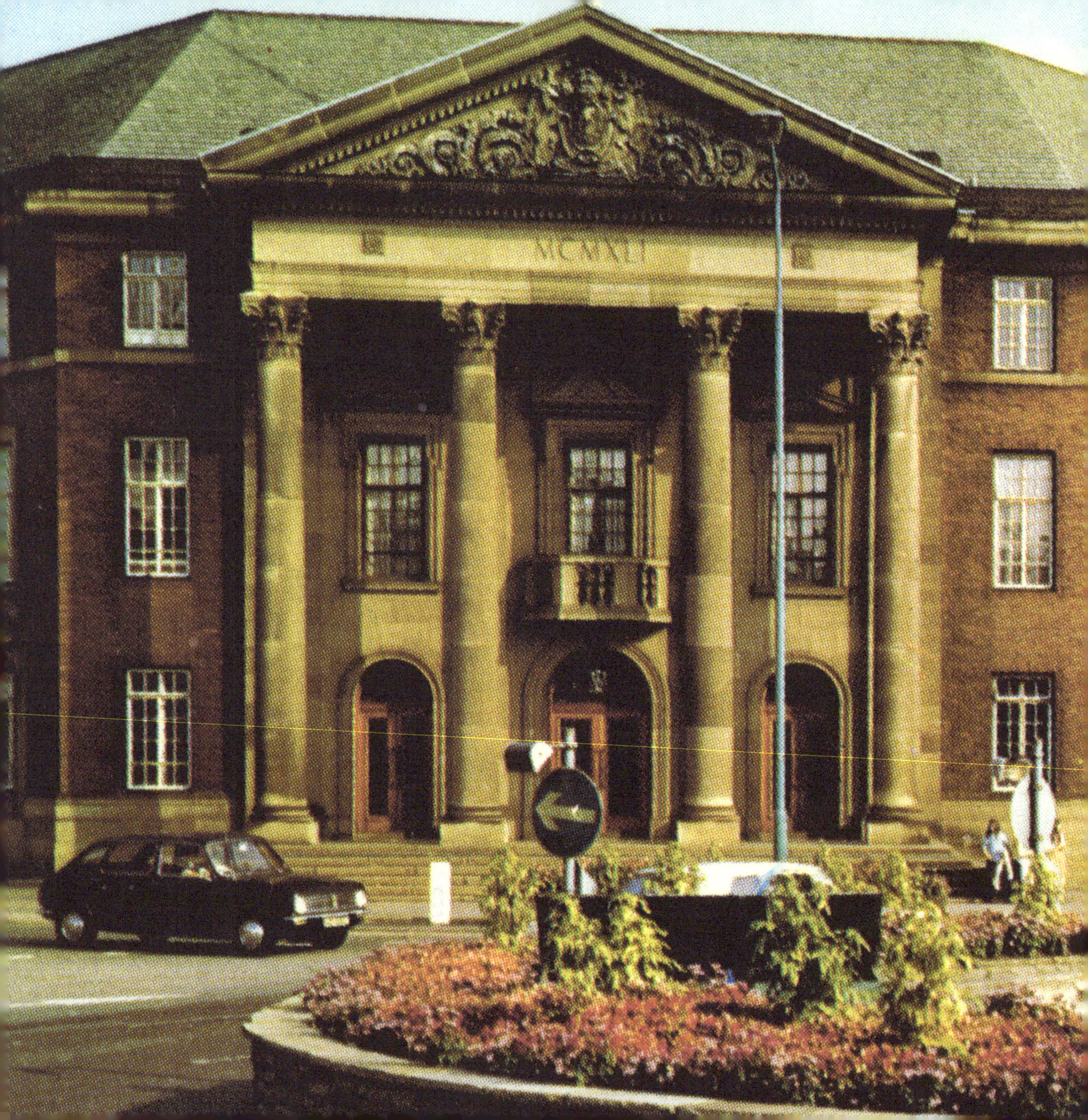

MCMXLI

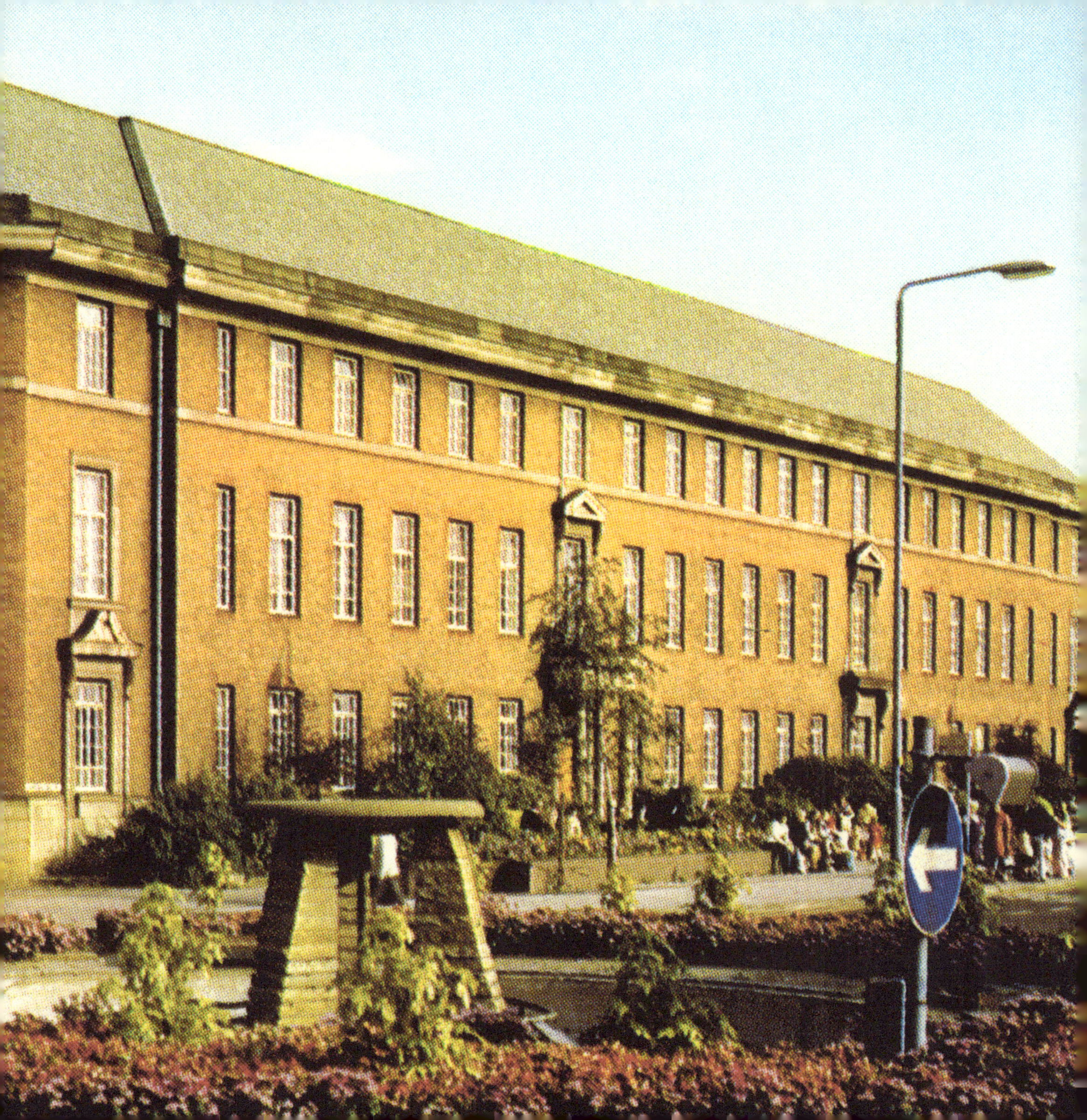

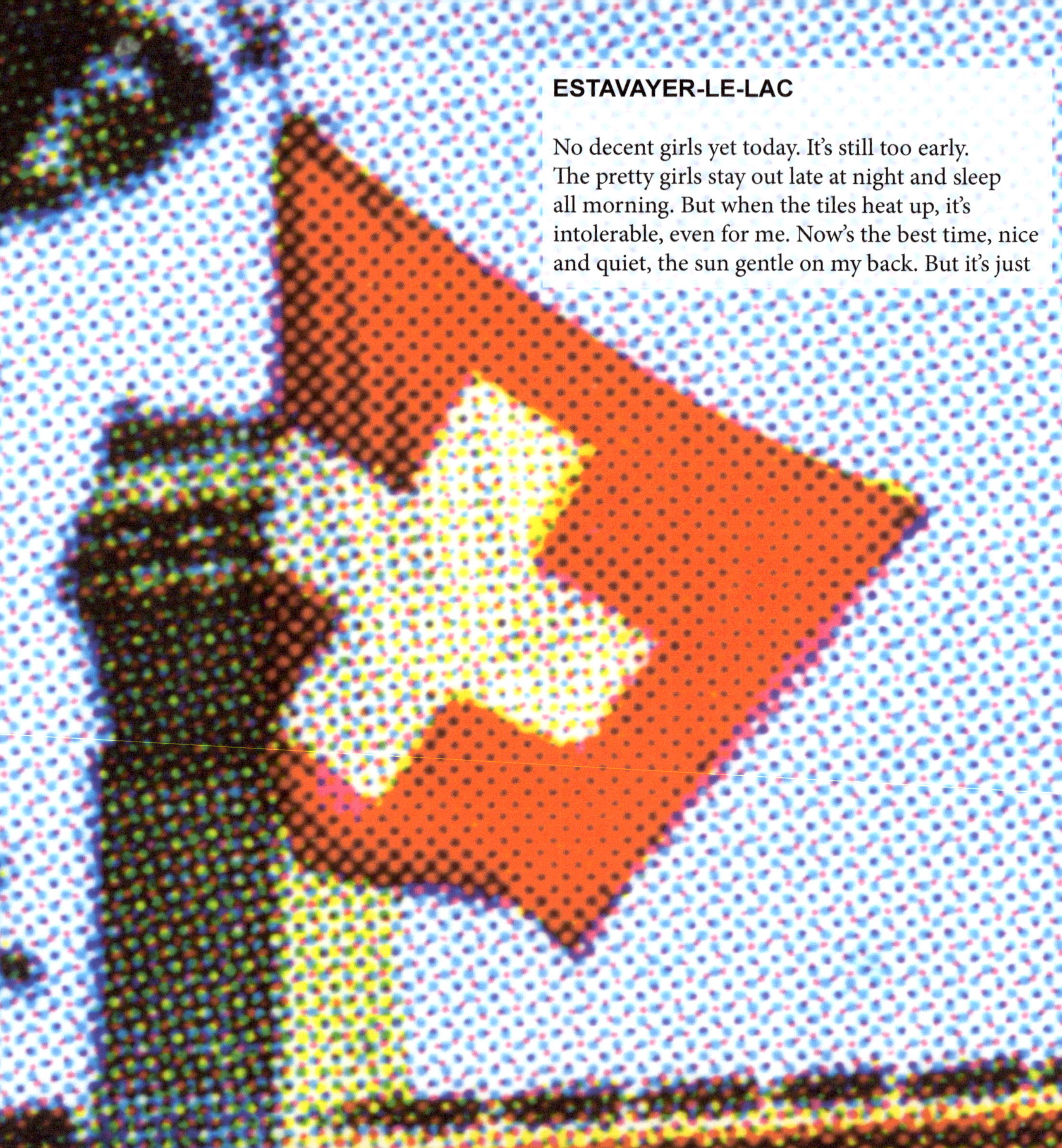
ESTAVAYER-LE-LAC

No decent girls yet today. It's still too early.
The pretty girls stay out late at night and sleep
all morning. But when the tiles heat up, it's
intolerable, even for me. Now's the best time, nice
and quiet, the sun gentle on my back. But it's just

kids down there, and their prunes of mothers.

No one looks up, or hardly ever. My God but it's boring down there. They just sit and stand, sit and stand. Sometimes they lie down. Sit and stand on the sand, then sit and stand in the water, come back and sit on the sand. Eating an ice cream is the most exciting it gets all day.

I can hear Mother. "Jean-Luc, Jean-Luc," all day long. Leave me alone. She can't get up here. She's scared of heights for one thing. And she's too fat to fit through the window for another. I'd like to see that. Now she's shouting to Father to go out and see if I'm up here. Yes, there he goes like a good dog. *Salut, Papa.* I'm not going to wave. What can they do?

Mother's just beneath the window unleashing one of her spiels. On and on and on. La la fucking la. Christ, there's some sort of photographer down there, with a big camera. Why's he taking photos of this dump? That's a job I wouldn't mind, going round with a camera taking pictures. Car accidents, girls, horse races, more girls, fires, storm damage – what a laugh. Mind you, look at that guy, taking a picture of this place. Hardly going to make his name doing that, is he? Nothing ever happens in this godforsaken country. Safest place in Europe. And the dullest.

What, she's got Father there now? What's he grunting on about? I'm not listening. I've heard it so many times before, I could probably recite it along with him. Why did you screw up at school? Why don't you get a job? Why don't you help around the place? Why do they bother saying it over and over? Is it my fault if they brought me into a world where nothing is worth any effort? Life goes on whether or not I sweep the floor or scoop ice creams for some old sow and her piglets.

Wait, they just pulled the window shut. That's the latch being fastened! *"Hey! Maman! Papa!"*

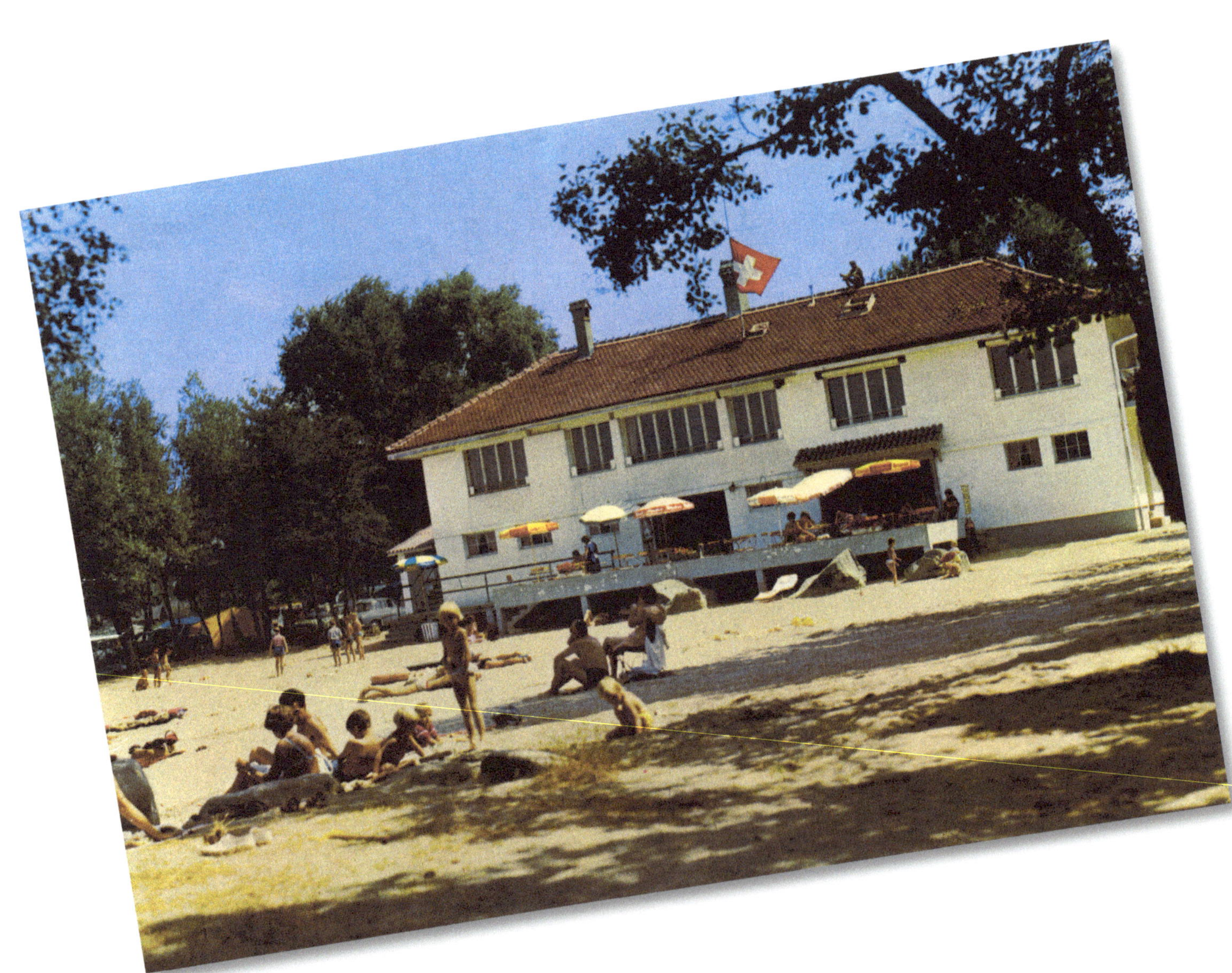

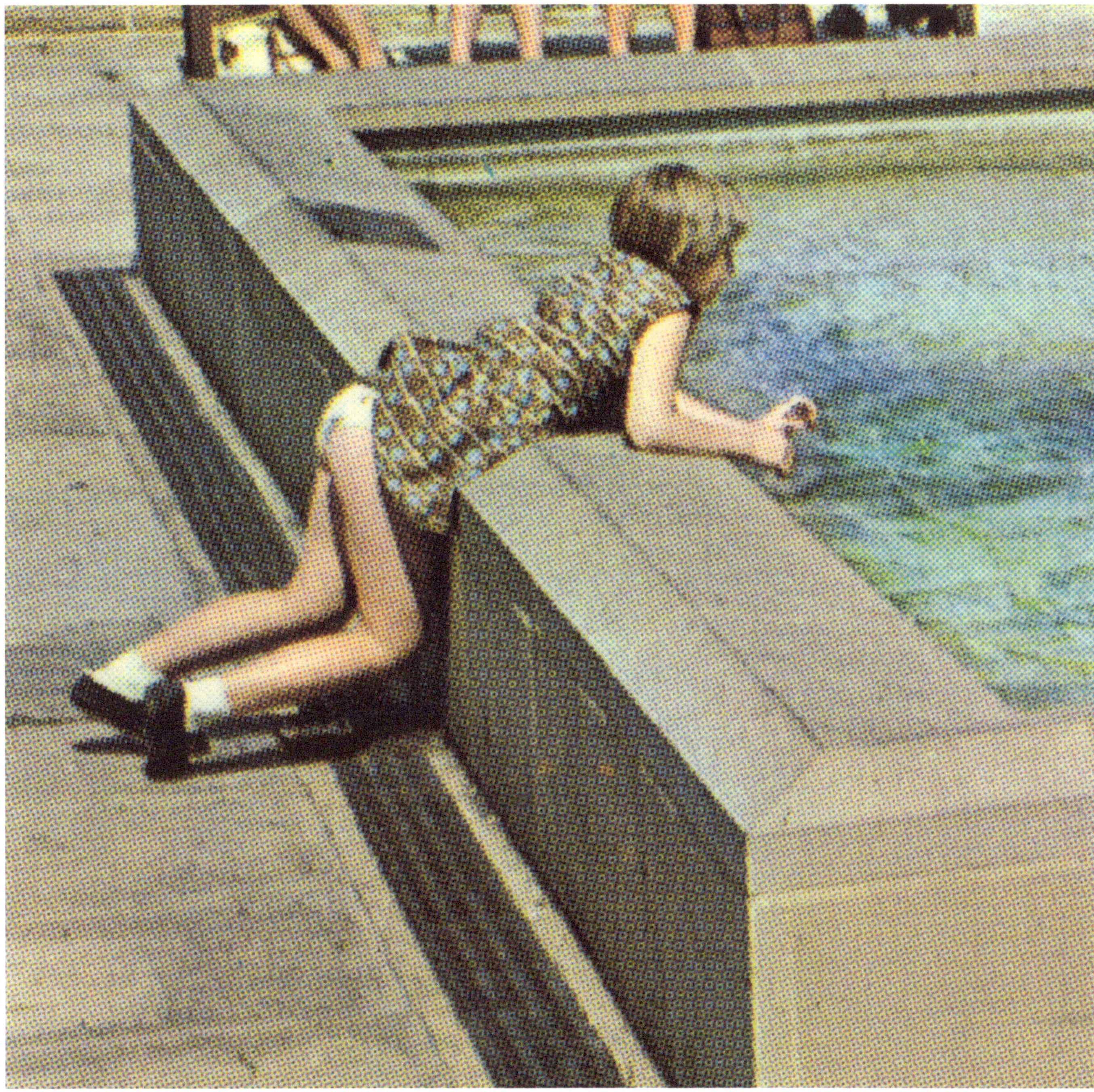

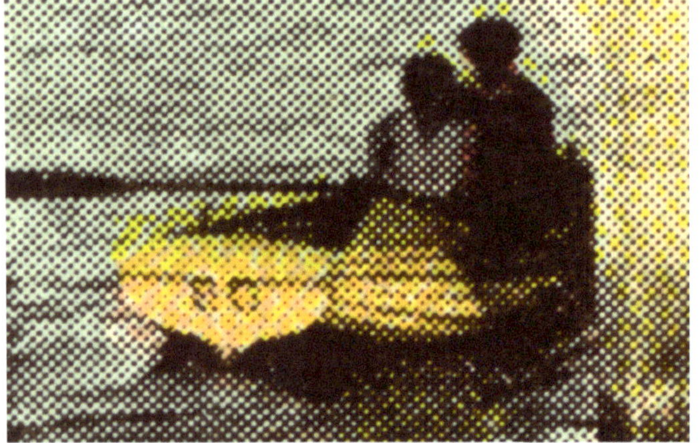

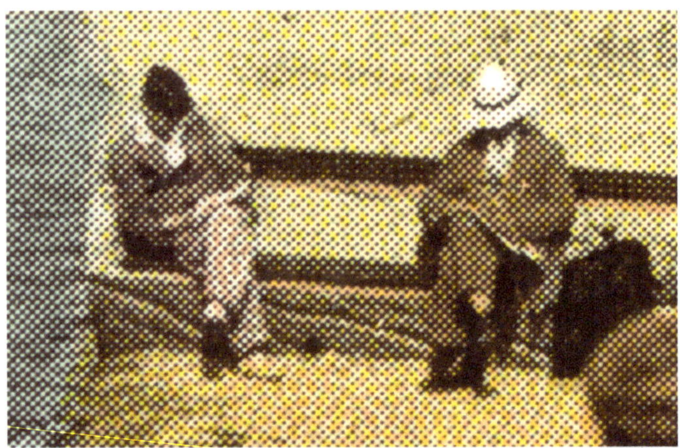

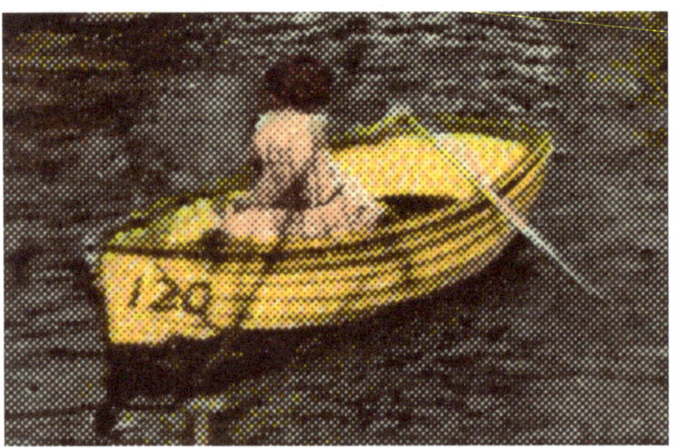

SKEGNESS

I had to bide my time, just like last year. Wait patiently until they were all caught up in their own concerns and then wait a bit longer still, just to be on the safe side. What if the time ran out and I had to just get back on the charabanc and go home? I couldn't miss this chance.

At last it seemed I wouldn't be missed. Mary Booth was tucked up in a row boat with George Harkness – we'd never hear the end of that now – while Sarah Tully was going round in circles on her own, trying to catch George's eye. What a fool she was making of herself, but it gave everyone else something to watch and whisper about. Margy and Kath were in the shelter, all agog. In truth the men were more interested in their racing tips. We were a dull bunch really and when the bus dropped us off at the boating lake no one had much thought to head off anywhere else. With luck there'd be a bit of warmth in the sun and it was a day away from Blenkiron's, maybe a chance for a bit of a flirt, a singsong on the way home – no one expected anything more. Except me.

Keeping my head down, I walked up to the path and then across the footbridge. I wasn't sure I could remember the way but once I got to the promenade I let my feet follow their memory and before long I recognised the road again, the red-brick church on the corner, the little newsagent's.

I hadn't been supposed to know that they had
moved to Skegness but I overheard Mother talking
to Aunt Grace about it and how she "hoped
that would be the end of it". Then, when I was at
Granny's that December I saw a Skegness address
on a Christmas card that was waiting to be posted.
It had to be them. It was Granny who had made
all the arrangements, Granny who had had me to
stay with her when I started to show and paid for
the nursing home when the time came. She told
my mother about an acquaintance of hers who was
desperate for a child. As I was the one who had
disgraced myself and shamed the family, I
forfeited any right to a say. The matter would be
dealt with and I should think myself lucky I had
'got away with it'. They took her off me when she
was a week old.

The works outing to Skegness is in July
every year – no one ever troubles themselves
to think of somewhere new to go. I got a job at
Blenkiron's almost as soon as I came back home.
I didn't care that the work bored me rigid. But
when the other girls told me about the day out –
giggling at the prospect of the amusements, the
opportunities for larks – I felt something inside
me snap to attention. I had that address
committed to memory, I said it to myself over and
over every night to make sure I didn't forget it. I
thought of her being there.

The first time I went I had to ask the way.
It wasn't too far from the Front. A nice street, the
houses tidy and quite new. I hadn't thought what
I was going to do. I just went there and walked
along until I came to the right house. Of course
I couldn't knock on the door, couldn't even stop

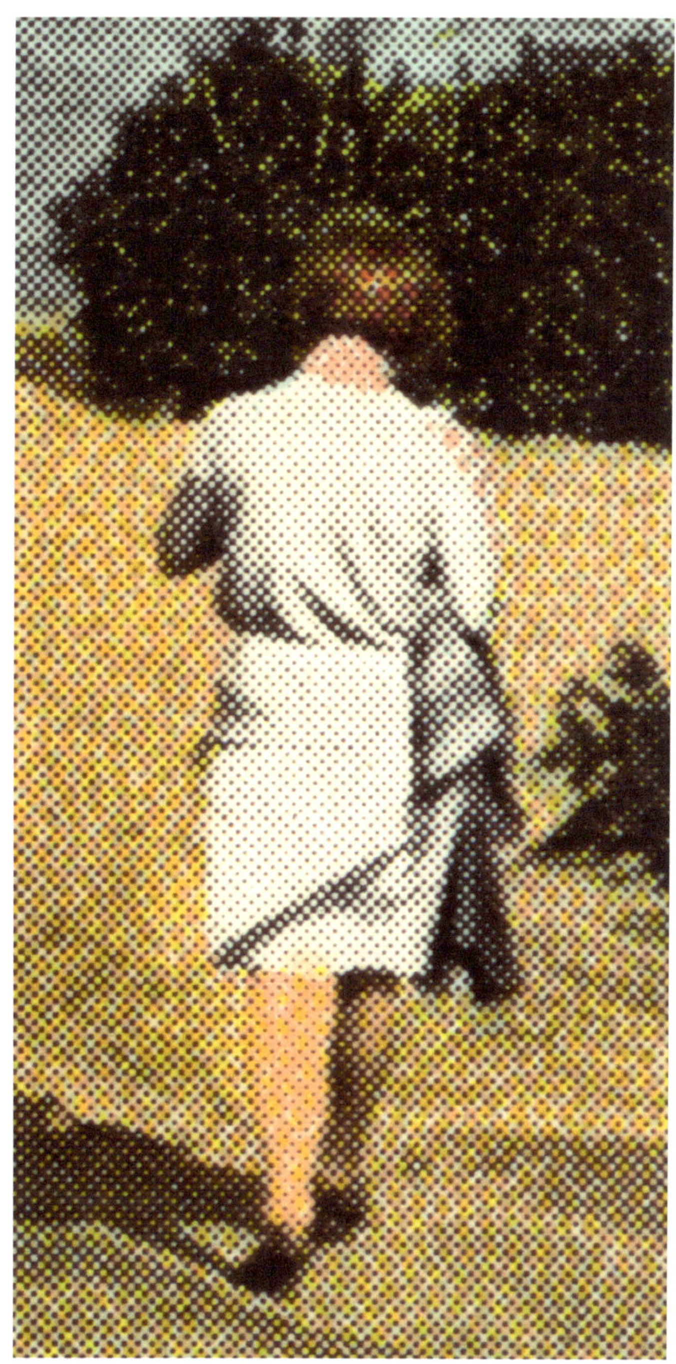

outside, so I glanced at it as I went past and kept going. It was nice enough, with thick white nets at the windows. I was terrified of being noticed so I walked on, a long way further on. Then I turned and came back down the road, as slowly as I dared.

I was nearly back at the start when I saw a woman coming towards me, pushing a big perambulator. She was nicely dressed, in a smart coat and hat. My heart started to beat so hard. It must be her. It must be. Before she drew level with me, before I had decided what I was going to do, she went into the newsagent's and I felt I couldn't follow her in there. I don't think she'd even noticed me. And maybe it wasn't even the right woman – God knows, there are enough people with babies in the world.

I had no idea how much time had passed but the sun had gone in and suddenly I felt afraid that I'd be missed. I hurried back and got the driver to let me wait in the bus until the others came. Said I'd taken poorly. Everyone was so giddy they barely noticed how quiet I was on the way home. Drunk as lords, most of them, by the time we got back, what with the stop at a pub in Market Rasen and the bottles of cheap brandy that some of the lads had in their back pockets.

Now a whole year had passed and I was back again, walking up the quiet road, a bit more sure of where I was going this time. I stayed on the other side of the street and didn't look around me too much on the way up, just a regular person out on an errand. When there were only a few more yards to go, I heard the click of a gate and the woman I had seen the last time came out of the house. I stopped, I couldn't help myself, and then, just behind her, a tiny figure appeared, all in white with little black boots. It was her and she was walking!

My hand flew to my mouth to try to stop myself from crying out but it was too late.

"Minnie!" That's the name I've given her. My Minnie.

Immediately the woman scooped my baby up and held her tightly to her chest. Her eyes flared. I heard a little squeak of protest from Minnie.

"You! Did you come here once before? Don't you dare come here ever again. You've no business here. You shouldn't ever have known to come here. I'll be having words with Mrs Graham about it, that's for sure…"

"Oh no, please, don't do that. She doesn't know I know. Can't I just…?"

"No you can't! There's no knowing what you might do. You don't look right. Go on, get away from here."

Minnie's sturdy little legs had begun to kick. I heard her say, "Mamma!"

The woman half ran back to her front door. She banged the door-knocker furiously and craned round to see if I was coming up behind her. I saw the door just opening as I turned and started walking away.

Ten, fifteen minutes at most and I was back at the boating lake. Kath and Margy were still in the shelter gossiping about everyone. George and Mary had gone off together, they said, so let's hope Mary had more sense than I did. Sarah Tully was sitting on her own on the other bank, playing the woman scorned.

"You all right, Annie? Where've you been all this time? You look like you've seen a ghost."

I mumbled something about a walk. One year. One year to plan. She'd be a really good walker by then. I would save every penny, starting right now. We'd catch a train somewhere. It would be hours before anyone missed me.

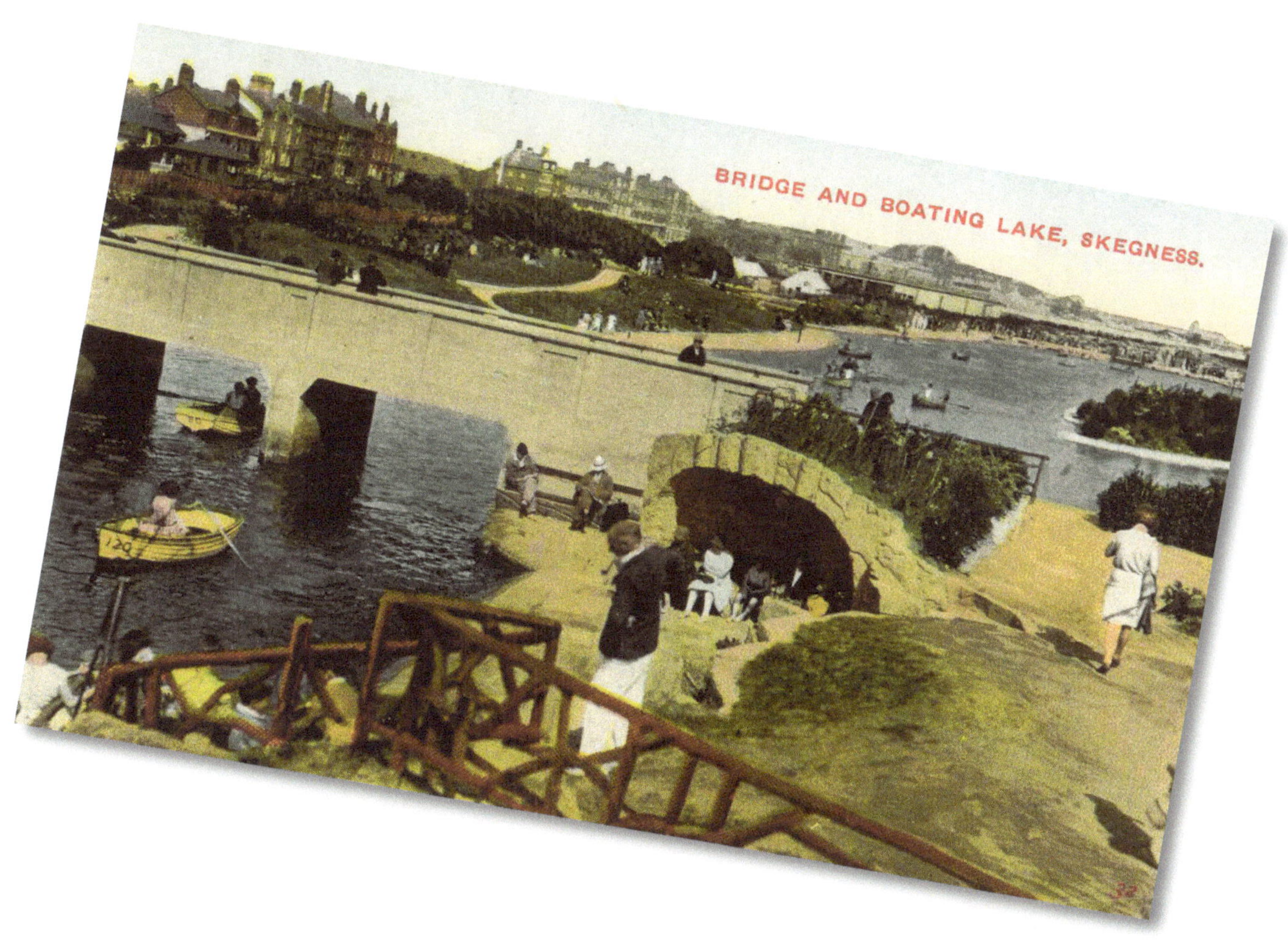

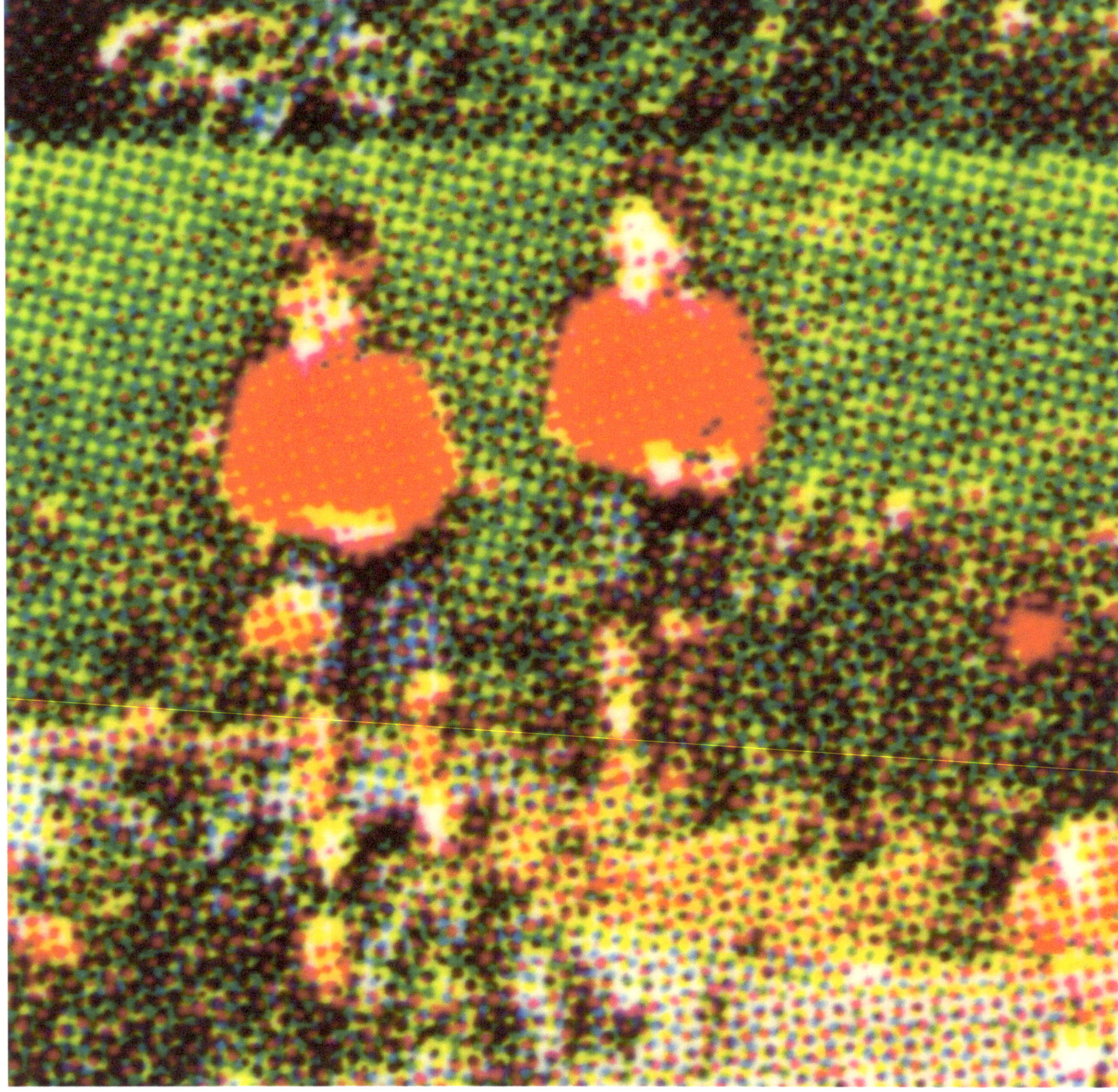

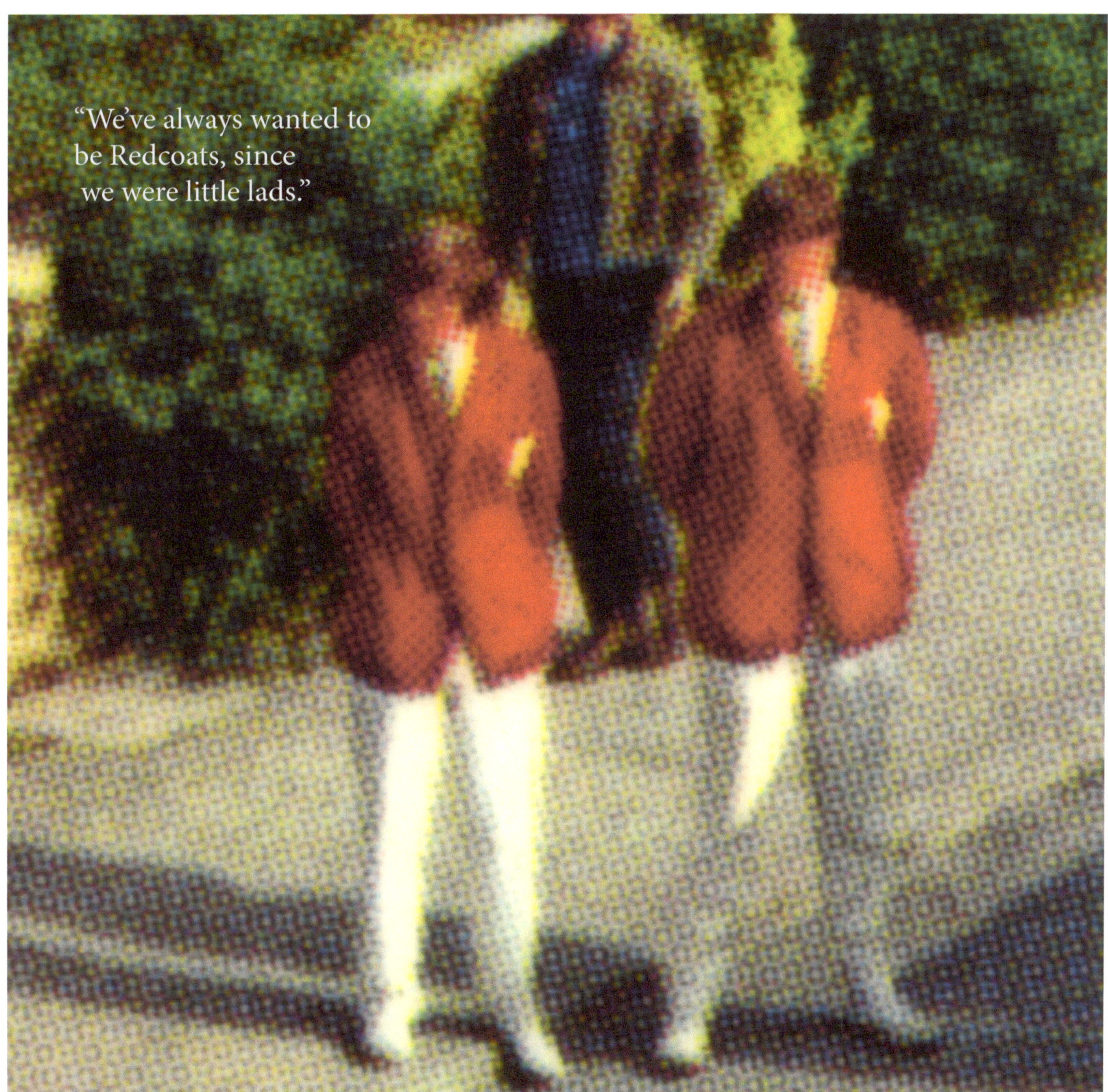

"We've always wanted to
be Redcoats, since
we were little lads."

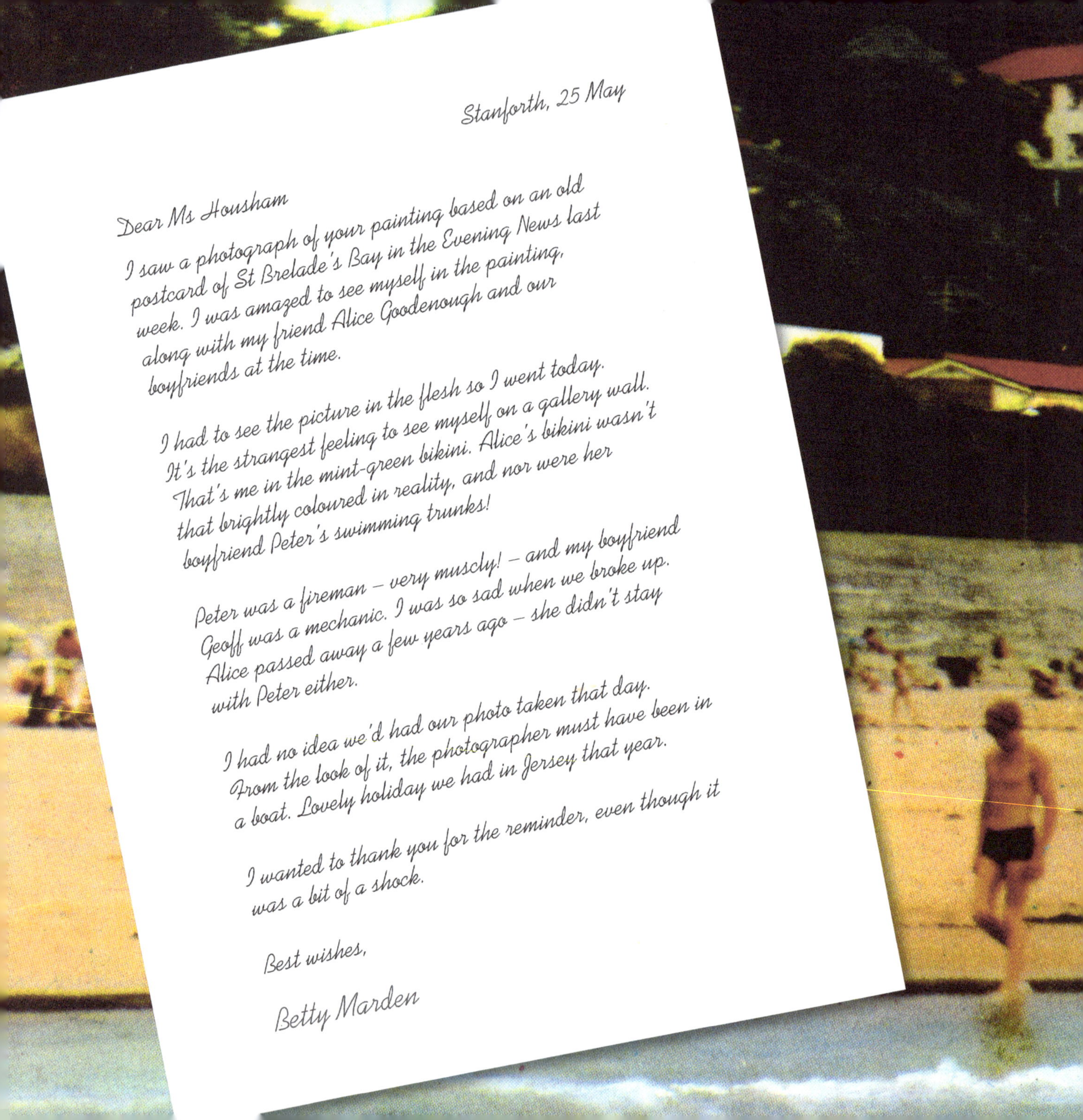

Stanforth, 25 May

Dear Ms Housham

I saw a photograph of your painting based on an old
postcard of St Brelade's Bay in the Evening News last
week. I was amazed to see myself in the painting,
along with my friend Alice Goodenough and our
boyfriends at the time.

I had to see the picture in the flesh so I went today.
It's the strangest feeling to see myself on a gallery wall.
That's me in the mint-green bikini. Alice's bikini wasn't
that brightly coloured in reality, and nor were her
boyfriend Peter's swimming trunks!

Peter was a fireman – very muscly! – and my boyfriend
Geoff was a mechanic. I was so sad when we broke up.
Alice passed away a few years ago – she didn't stay
with Peter either.

I had no idea we'd had our photo taken that day.
From the look of it, the photographer must have been in
a boat. Lovely holiday we had in Jersey that year.

I wanted to thank you for the reminder, even though it
was a bit of a shock.

Best wishes,

Betty Marden

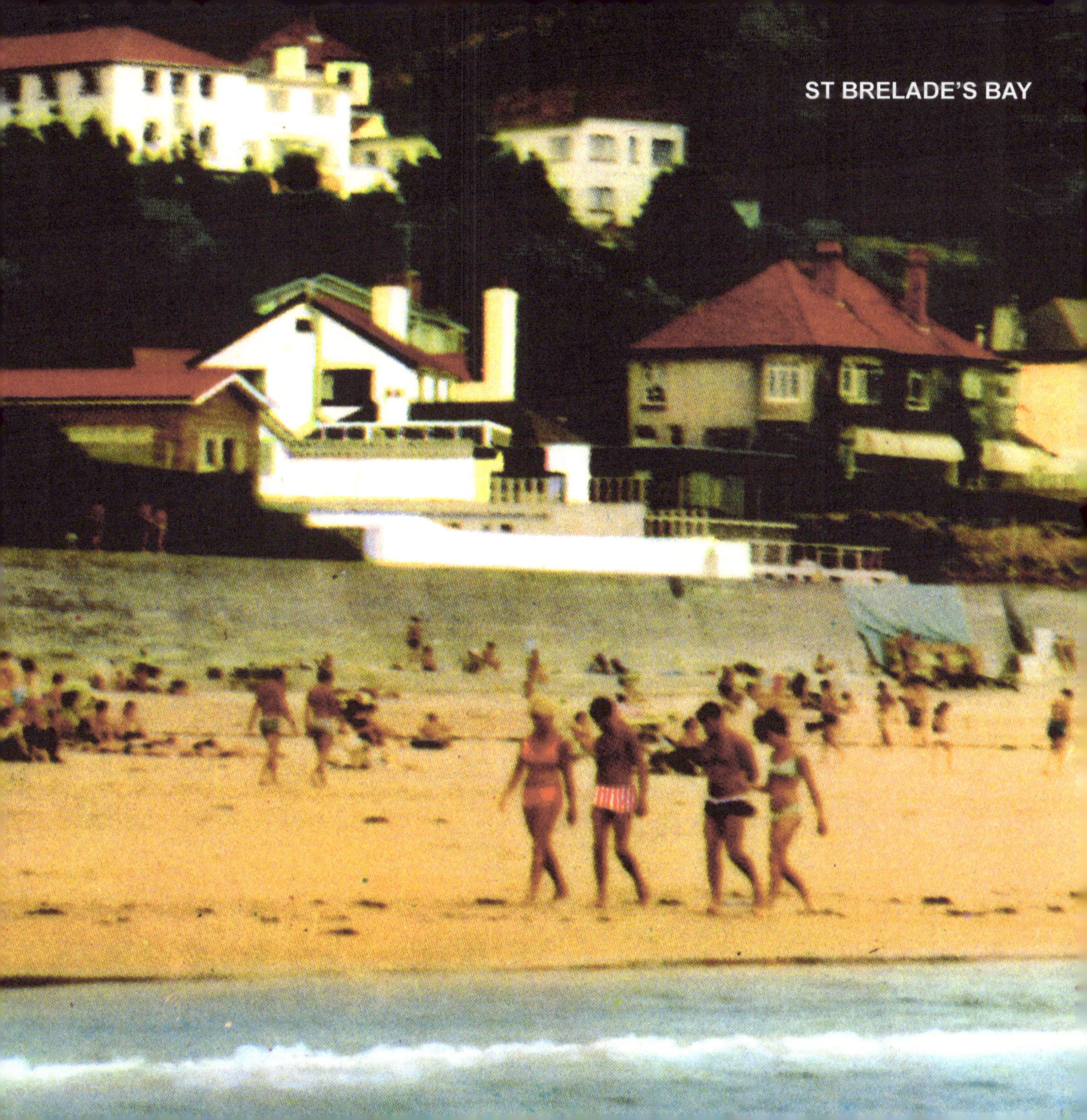
ST BRELADE'S BAY

REDCAR

Patty! Patty's there, just there, in a boat with a lad. Who's she with? He's not looking this way, neither's she. She looks happy. He's going to get that suit wet, the way he's going on, looking for a splashing from that other boat. Some lads want everything to be a fight, even if it's just a laugh. Not me, but if he sees me looking at Patty…

Who's she waving at? Not me. She hasn't even seen me. That's good, I suppose. She's going to see me in a second, though. What'll she do? She looks happy. Had her hair done, by the look of it. She must be on a date with that lad. Not much of a date, going on the boats, but she looks happy enough. If you like a lad, you don't care that much where you go with them, do you? Or a lass.

Claire's had her hair done too. Dyed red – auburn, she called it – and set like a massive ball. It smells like ICI, makes me sneeze. When we get round to the car park we're going to have to decide what we're going to do. She's still crying. I wish Patty would smile at me. I could just say her name, quite quiet, and she'd hear it. So would he, though. Looks like they're coming in, any road. That kid's going to pull them in. Probably waiting for a turn. Better if we keep walking. I wouldn't like Claire to see Patty when she's in this state. She might start screaming at her. No reason to, but then, when does she need a reason? I'm between her and Patty. We'll just keep walking.

Bye, Patty. Did you see it was me? Do you miss me? Are you watching me walk away from you? I suppose you won't want the lad to see you looking at me. Maybe I'll see you out tonight? I'll ask you if you saw me by the boating lake. You probably won't want to talk to me.

"Yes, love, sorry, what was that? Don't worry about the hanky, you hang on to it. Soon be back at the car. No, no one saw you leaving, I'm sure of it."

Christ, now I'm in trouble. I haven't been listening to a word she's been saying. We were at her sister's wedding, at the Coatham Hotel, when all of a sudden she says, "Let's go, we've got to go." So we did. I wasn't that bothered about leaving. Her sister's a right stuck-up cow. We'd had the grub – nothing special – and they'd done the speeches. I was laying into my third pint. Then I feel Claire pulling at my sleeve, looking like she's seen a ghost.

"Let's go," she says, so off we go, back to my car. Didn't think I'd be driving again till tonight, give me time to sober up. Maybe if we sit in the car for a bit, she'll be alright.

I haven't the foggiest idea why we had to leave like that. I can't face a whole afternoon of dealing with it. If I drop her at her mother's maybe I can come back and find Patty again. Make it look like chance, kind of thing.

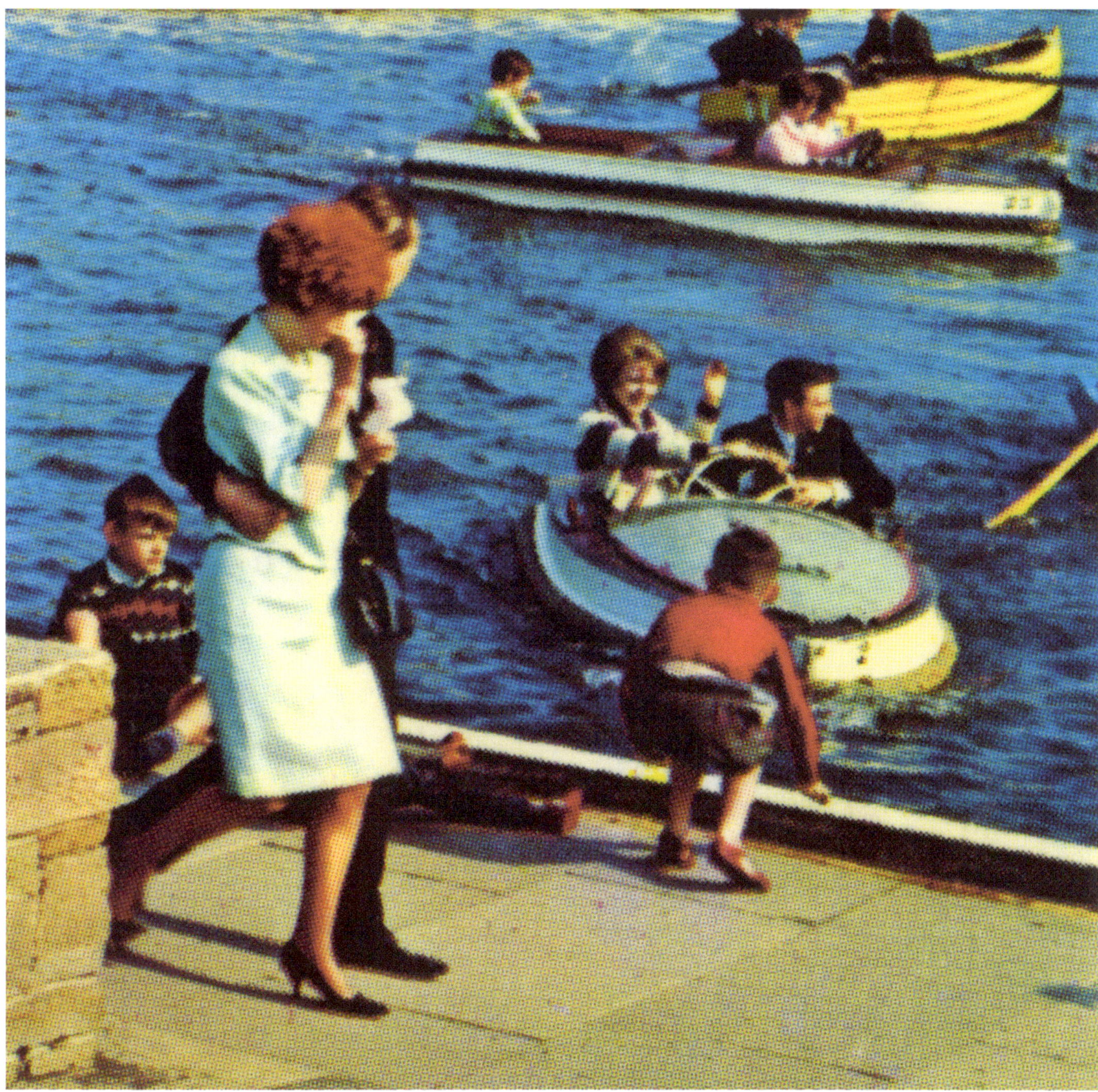

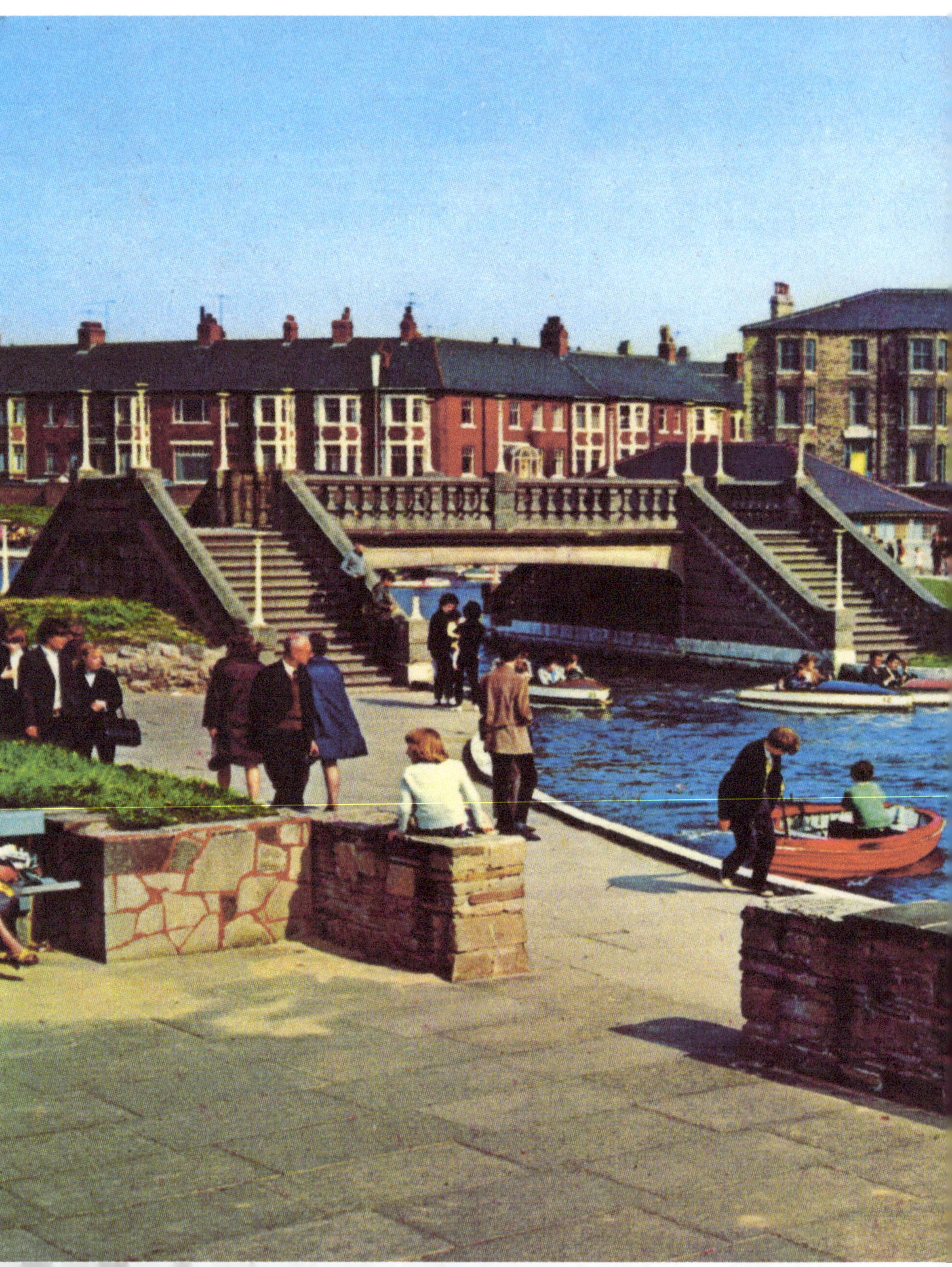

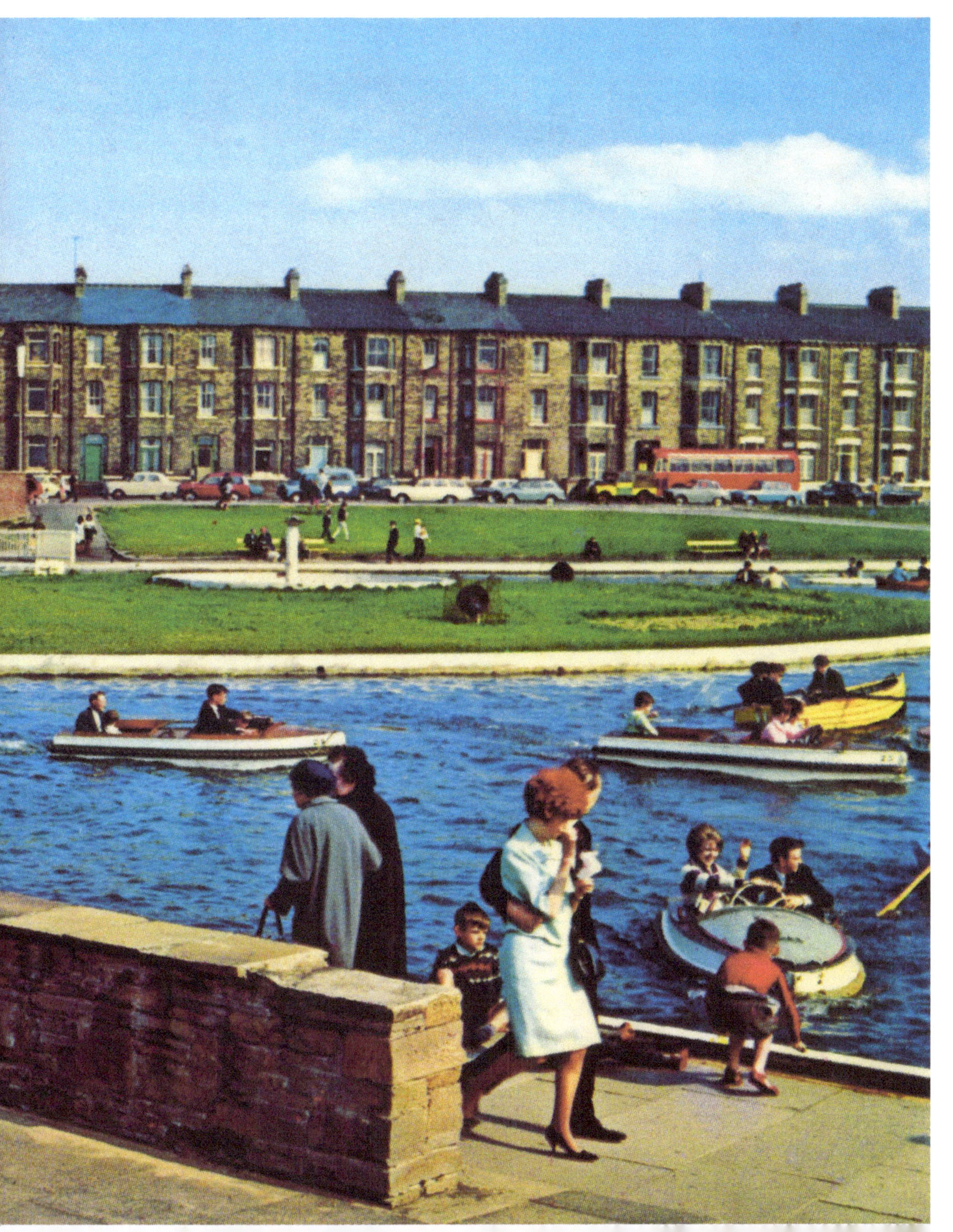

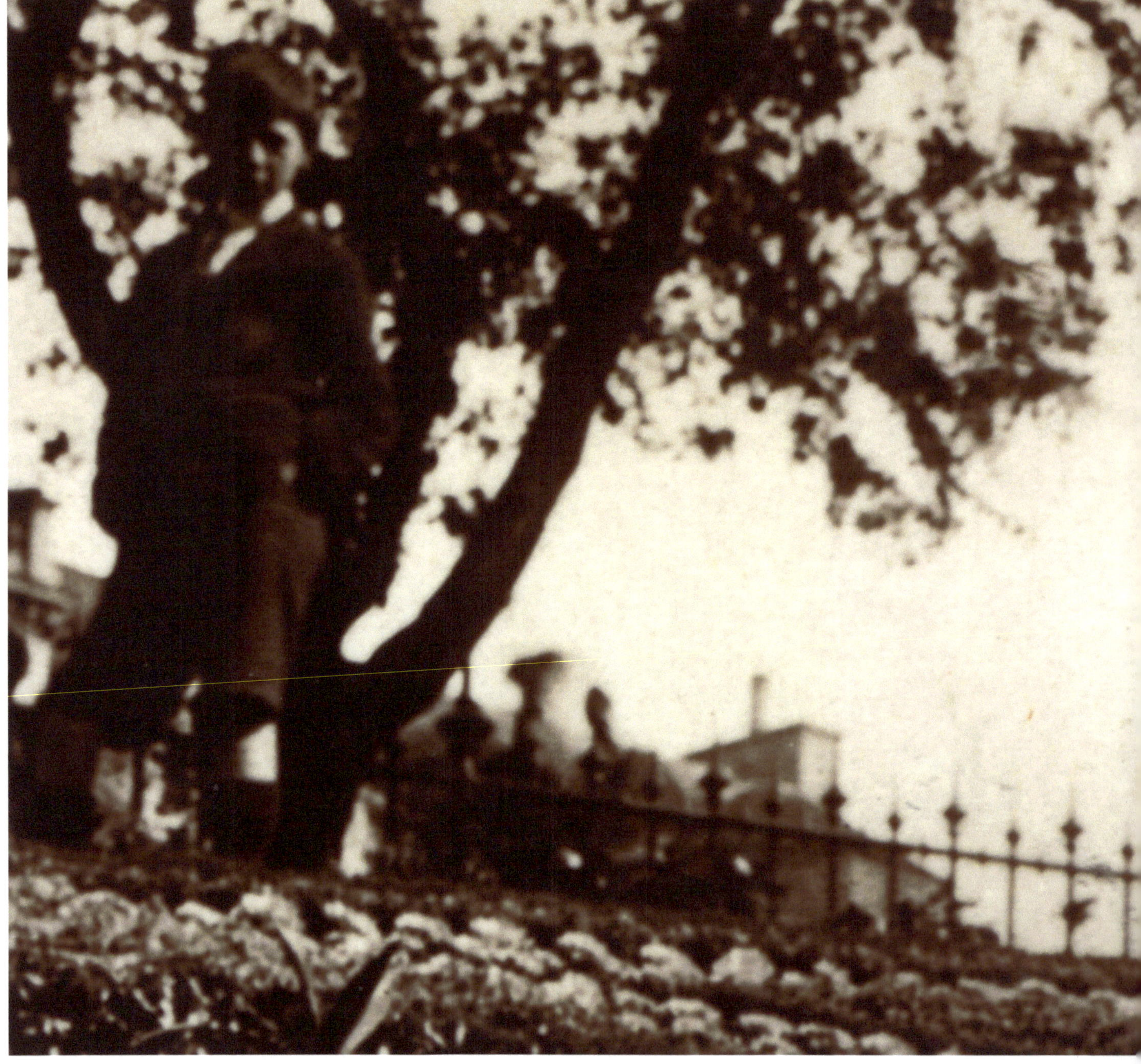

EDINBURGH

I'm going to get my picture and get out of here. The angle's all wrong anyway.

"Make sure you get the Floral Clock," they said to me in the office before I set off up here, "We always sell more of that than anything else, apart from Greyfriars Bobby." Well, I've got the dog, and the Castle, the Mound, Arthur's Seat, you name it. Everything apart from the ruddy clock. I came yesterday but it was being tidied up and there were two men crawling all over it on ladders weeding it, so I couldn't get my picture. Now I'm here, with my train to catch at ten. Should be able to get my shot and away.

I don't like the look of that kid. Nor those blokes gathering behind him. More and more keep coming to stare. I should be used to it by now and, anyway, it's the main street just up there. Stands to reason there's going to be onlookers. But I don't like being stared at. Puts me off. And I don't like the look in that kid's eye, like he's just waiting for me to put my eye to the camera and he'll be down to snatch my suitcase before you can say knife.

Ha, but if he thinks about it for two seconds, he'll maybe realise that in a moment I'm going to have his picture safely in the bag. If he does me a mischief I'll have his picture in the post to the editor of *The Scotsman* within the week and then we'll see who's the boss of Edinburgh. There, got you, you little monster.

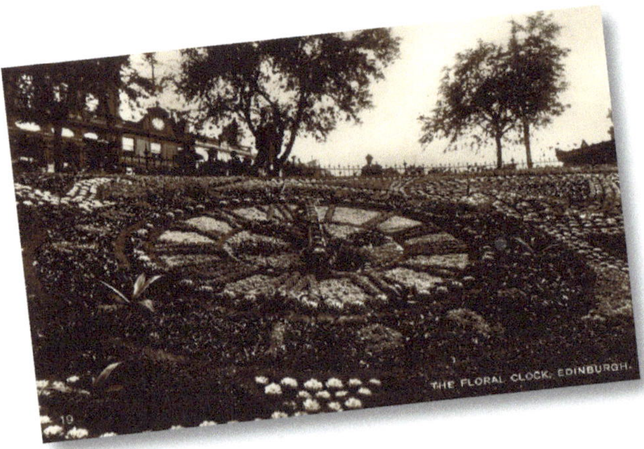

"Hey, what the…!" Damnation! Another kid's away with my case, crept up behind me!

"Stop, thief! Stop that kid, for goodness' sake!" I don't believe this is happening. I can't run with the camera. The little bastard's got away with my clothes, damn him. "And you can all stop your laughing too!"

I'm going for the train. At least I have my shots safe in the camera bag. I'm never coming back to this damned city.

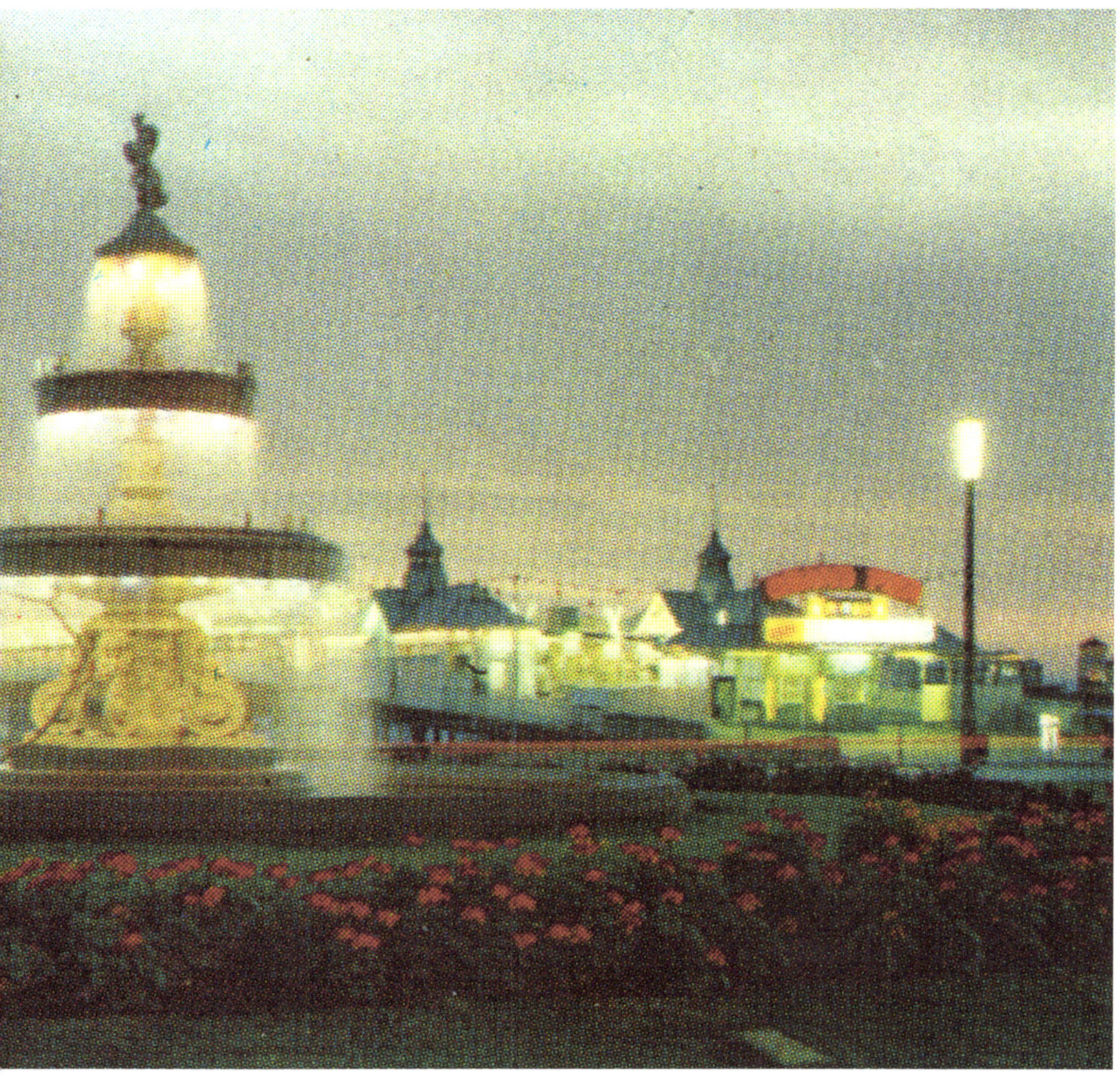

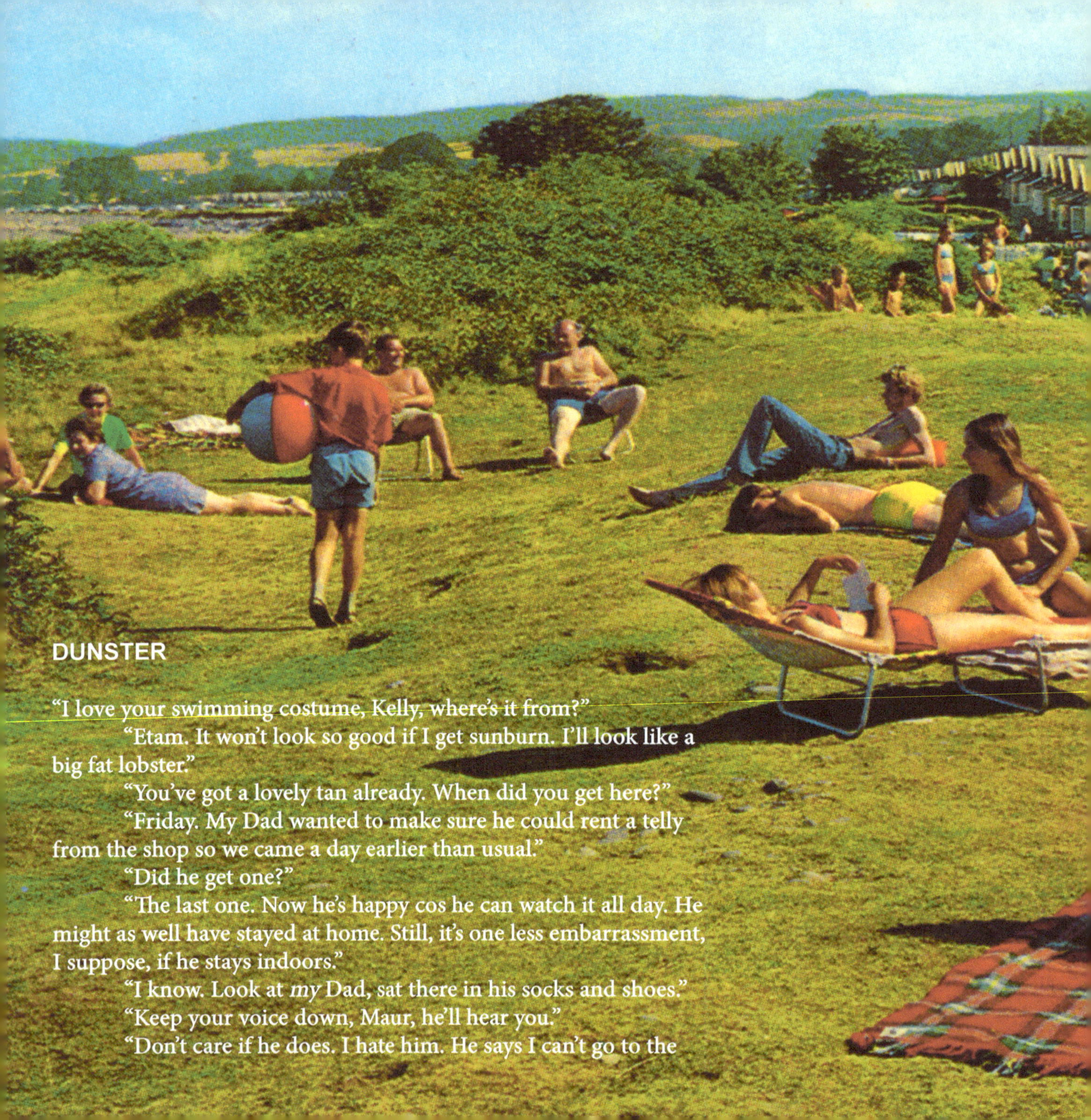

DUNSTER

"I love your swimming costume, Kelly, where's it from?"

"Etam. It won't look so good if I get sunburn. I'll look like a big fat lobster."

"You've got a lovely tan already. When did you get here?"

"Friday. My Dad wanted to make sure he could rent a telly from the shop so we came a day earlier than usual."

"Did he get one?"

"The last one. Now he's happy cos he can watch it all day. He might as well have stayed at home. Still, it's one less embarrassment, I suppose, if he stays indoors."

"I know. Look at *my* Dad, sat there in his socks and shoes."

"Keep your voice down, Maur, he'll hear you."

"Don't care if he does. I hate him. He says I can't go to the

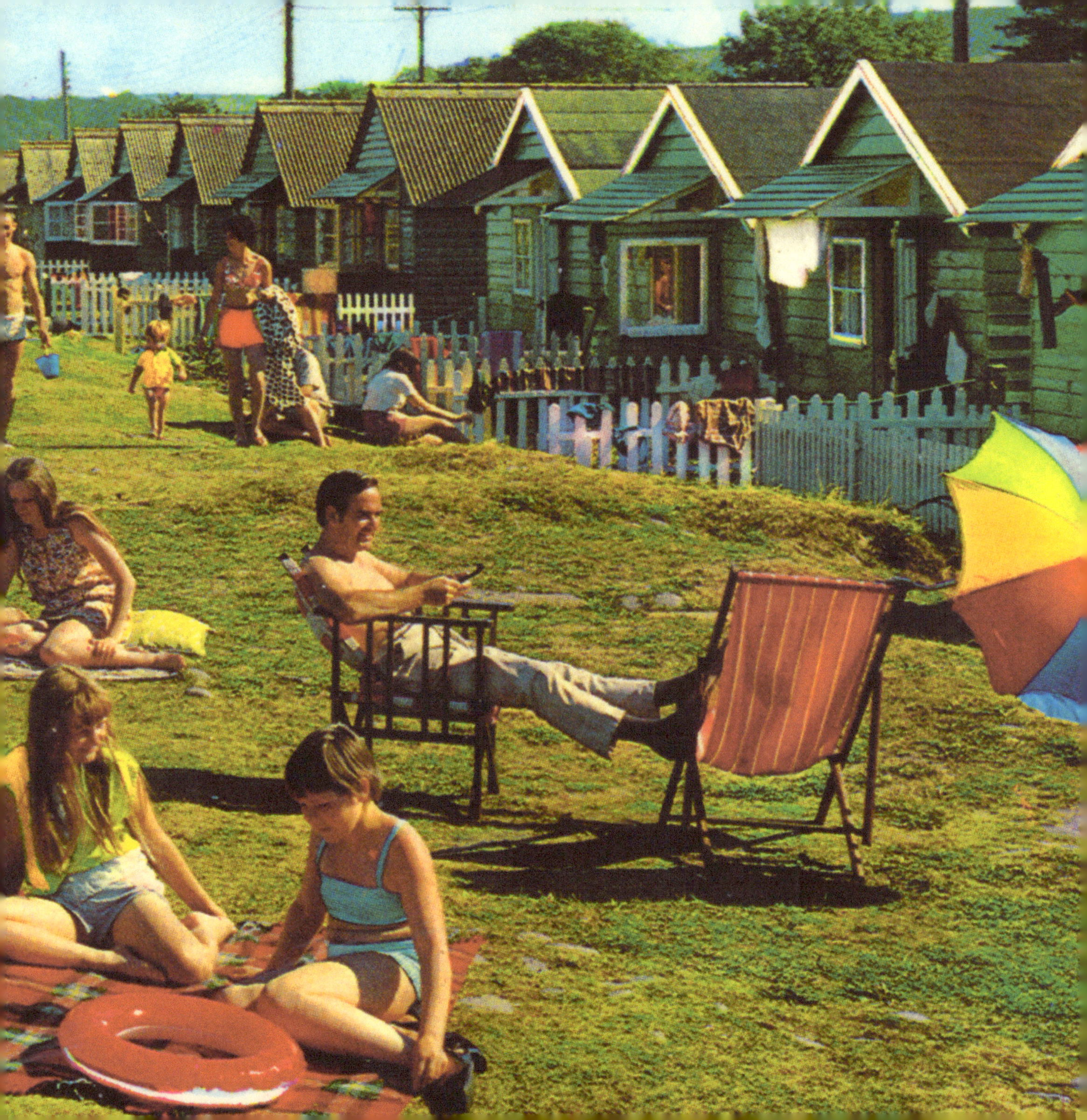

disco in Minehead."

"Aw no, he didn't? He'll come round, won't he?"

"Maybe. I still hate him. Always passing comments about me."

"What sort of comments?"

"Like I shouldn't wear short skirts and to cover up on top and that."

"Poor you. Is that why you haven't got your cozzie on?"

"Sort of. I just don't feel ready for all the stares and carry on."

"I know what you mean."

"What's that you're reading, Kelly?"

"Nothing."

"Go on, it's a letter. Who's it from?"

"Nobody."

"It can't be from nobody."

"It is, a real nobody."

"Tell us who it's from. We only come down here every year to catch up with you. Nothing half as exciting ever happens to us as it does to you, Kel. Isn't that so, Sharon?"

"Nope, not a thing. Unless you count a girl at school nicking one of my sausages right out of my tray at lunch last week."

"Ooh, I'd've killed her."

"It was the school bully, she's too scary. Anyway, your letter's more interesting than that."

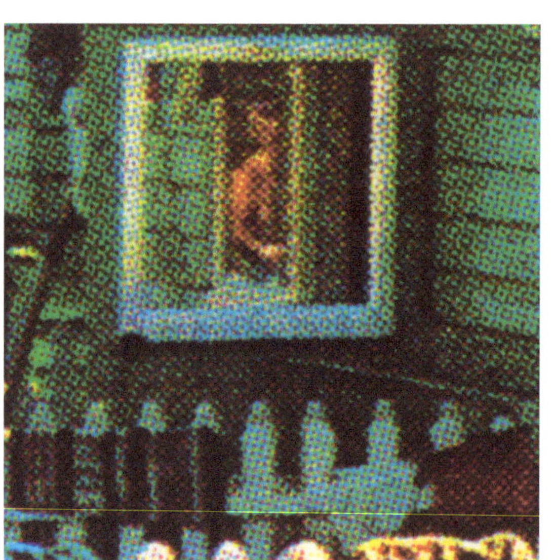

"It just came this morning, Mr Thackeray brought it round from the post office. I gave Michael the address here so he could send me something romantic, tell me he missed me or something, and he's only gone and finished with me."

"What a rotten coward, waiting till you were on holiday."

"I know. It's such an awful letter, too, his writing's like a six-year-old's and he can't spell 'embarrassing'. Or 'laughing'."

"Why's he said those words?"

"He says it was 'embarsing' when I danced with Leo Marks at the end-of-term disco and he saw people 'laufing' at him."

"And did you dance with Whatsisname?"

"Leo? Only cos he asked me."

"Do you like him?"

"Who, Michael?"

"No, this Leo."

"Not really, he's a bit on the short side. No, honestly, I'm glad Mike's dumped me because now I won't feel guilty if anything happens down here."

"Ooh, like what?"

"Well… no, nothing."

"Don't tease us!"

"Don't turn round, but… I said *don't* turn round…"

"I can't help it. Anyway, go on."

"There's a boy behind you. Levi's. Longish hair. Sideburns. I really like his sideburns."

"I want to see him! Was he there before? I didn't see any lads worth looking at when we came out."

"He just came along now and sat down. But I saw him last night in the shop. He keeps looking over here."

"I really want to see what he's like."

"Well, get up and fetch something from your chalet, then you can get a good look at him. Oh bloody hell, no, don't."

"What?"

"I can see your Mum in your chalet."

"Oh, she's all right. She's a laugh, most of the time."

"She's in the nuddy."

"Kelly, no! You're having me on."

"Swear to God, Sharon. I can't see her bottom half but I can see her… whatsits."

"I'll never live this down, Kelly. Is everybody looking?"

"Don't think so. No one's noticed except me. Oh, it's all right, she was just putting her swimsuit on. Oh flaming Nora."

"What is it now? Has she got them out again?"

"No, it's just I've been giving that guy with the sideburns the eye, but there's a kid in front of

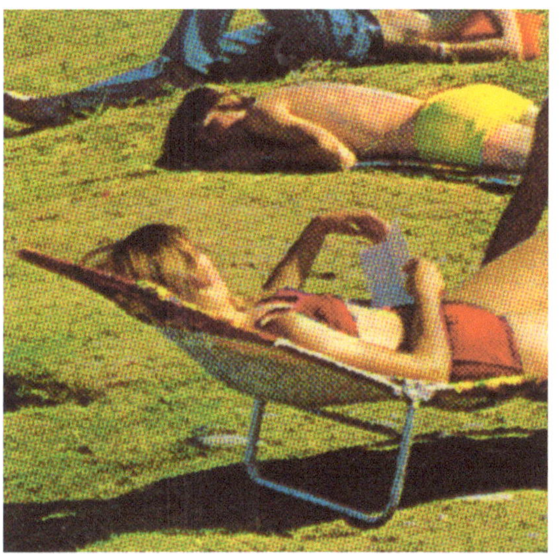

him – no, don't look, you'll only encourage him – and now he's staring at me all gooey-eyed. I think he thinks I fancy *him*."

"That's Stacey Simon's kid brother, from Wolverhampton. They come every year like us but he's grown huge compared to last year."

"Oh no, he's got yellow swimming trunks on. That's the pits."

"He's only about twelve."

"Let's go down to the beach and see if that guy comes down too. We can start building a bonfire for tonight, like last year, by the pillbox. It might all get wild and sexy again."

"Wild and sexy! Stacey Simon thought she might fall for a baby, it was awful. Don't you remember the state she was in?"

"No, I thought it was brilliant. Come on, let's go down there anyway. But if that kid comes trailing after us I'm going to kick sand in his face."

"Aw, Kelly, don't be rotten."

"I mean it."

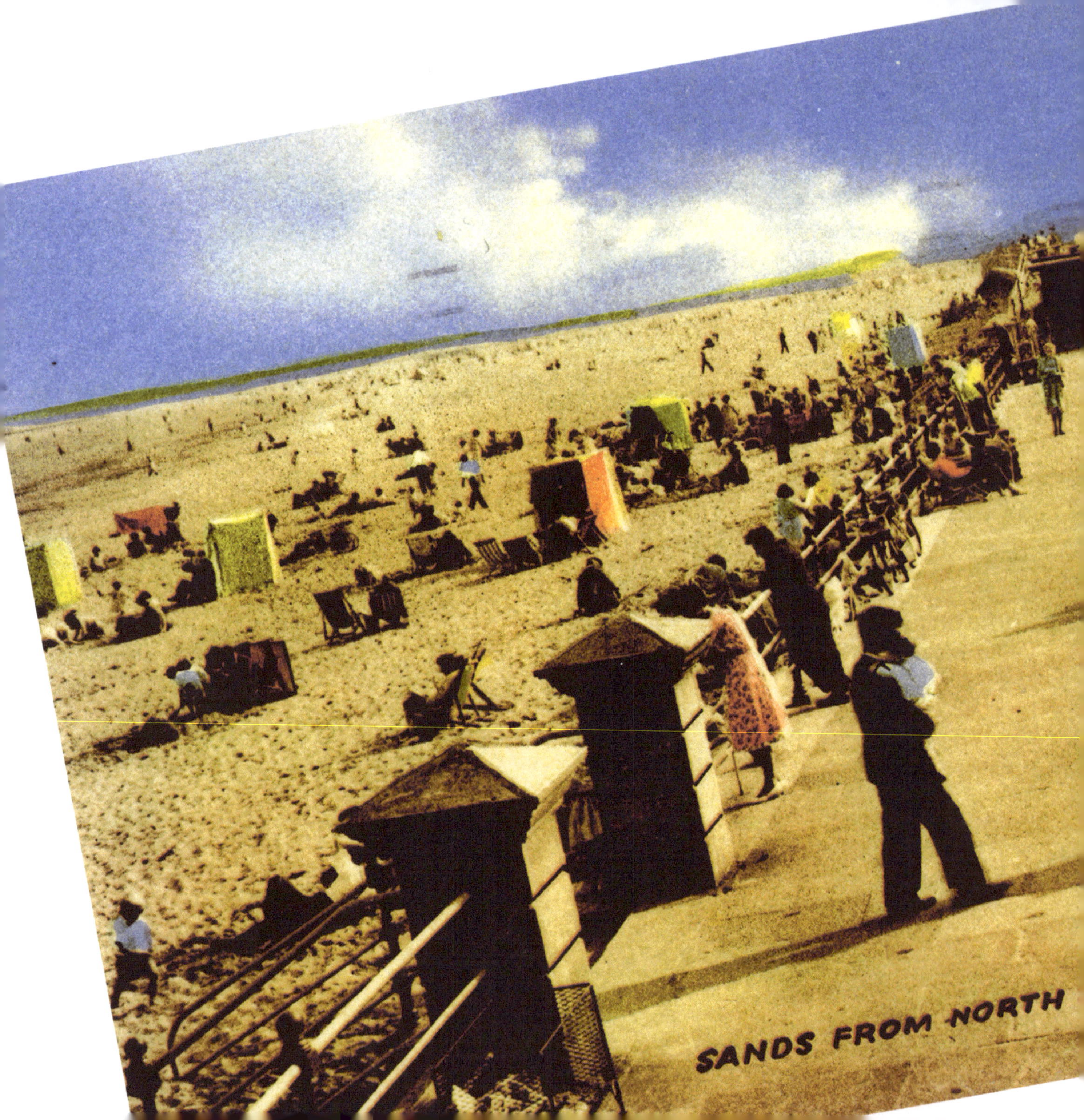

SANDS FROM NORTH

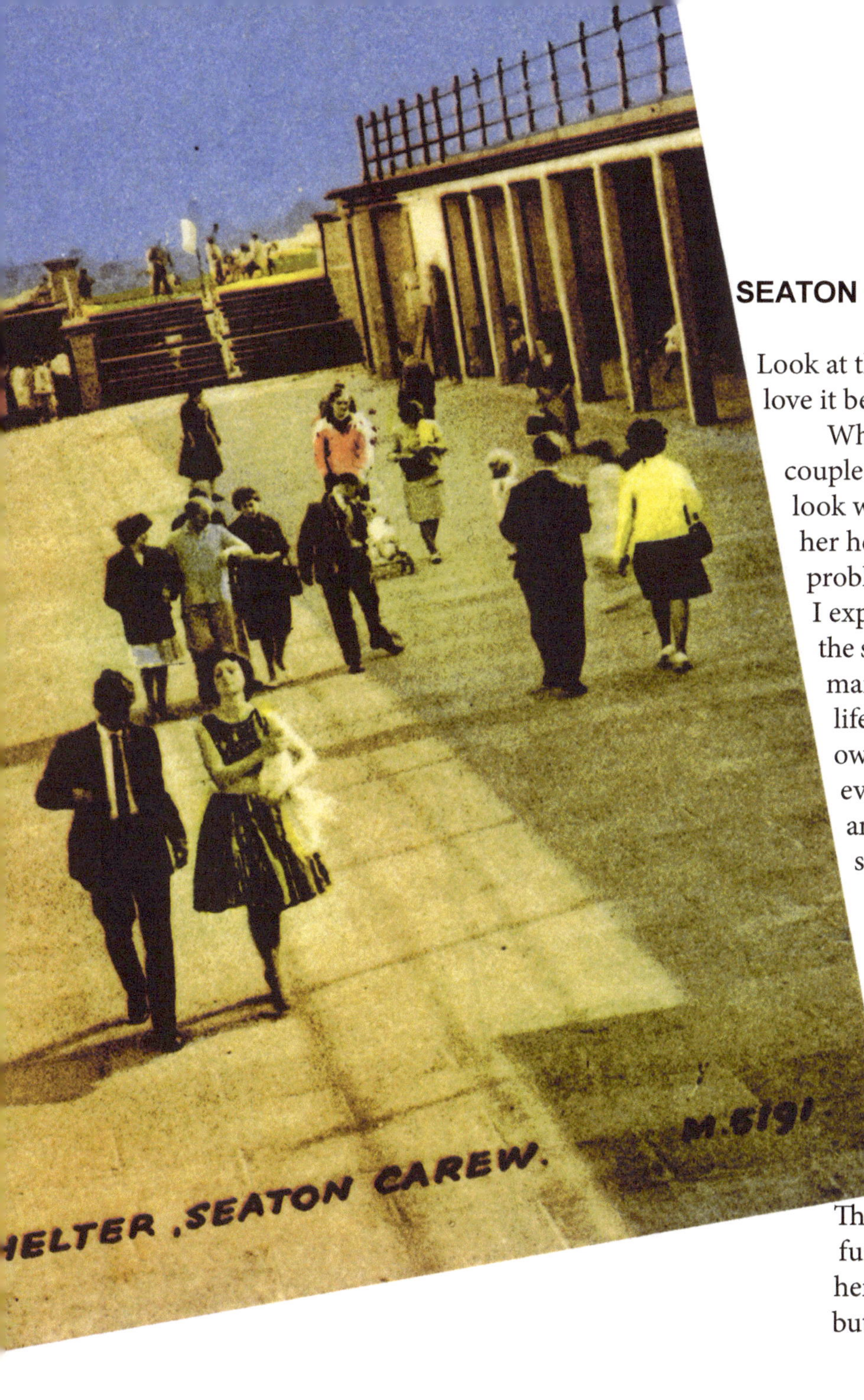

SEATON CAREW

Look at this card. It's one of my favourites. I love it because it seems to be full of stories.

What have we got? There's the young couple striding along towards us. They look wonderful, almost French, her with her head held so high. High heels but no problem walking in them, lived in them, I expect. I think they're on a day out by the seaside, still courting but destined to marry. They have high hopes for their life together. I think they're like my own parents, keen to take advantage of everything life could offer them in the ambitious Sixties. They have an aura of self-belief.

Then there's the man carrying the child across the picture. Is that his child? Could he be taking it? Is the little boy on the far left trying to follow him, shouting to his parents that a man's taken the baby? Almost certainly not but we're in the business of spinning tales here.

There's a very slender lady much further back. She's just standing on her own, looking very contained but also terribly lonely. What's her

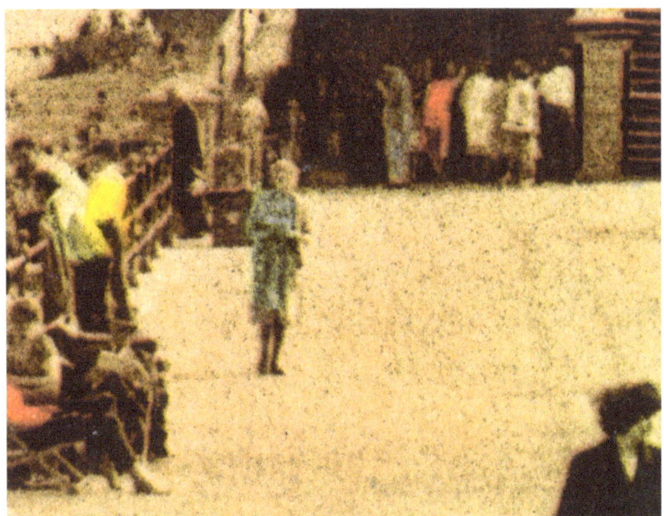

story? Being on your own is much worse at the seaside, where you're supposed to have fun, to have company. Perhaps the lady in the dark dress is walking away from her in a huff because they've had a falling out?

And is there a man in the middle who's worried he's stepped in dog dirt?

I also like the tiny flash of white in the top right, behind the pillars, that's a little girl running. I'm sure she isn't running *away*, but I always like to catch glimpses of children running. Their energy brings postcards to life.

There's so very little to be said for this card in terms of the view: the great sweep of sand, but no sea in sight (unless that thin, wobbly line in the distance is supposed to be the sea). The concrete expanse of the esplanade is exactly the same colour as the sand. Then there are the utilitarian pillars and the spacious shelters, surely needed very frequently against the rain. The object closest to the viewer is a large rubbish bin which it might

have been nice to crop out. The art department girls have crudely touched up the picture with a minimum of colours, just acid yellow and salmon pink, but it has had the effect of uniting the different elements in the image and making it thoroughly harmonious. For me, this card is all about the people, especially the young couple striding confidently through their domain.

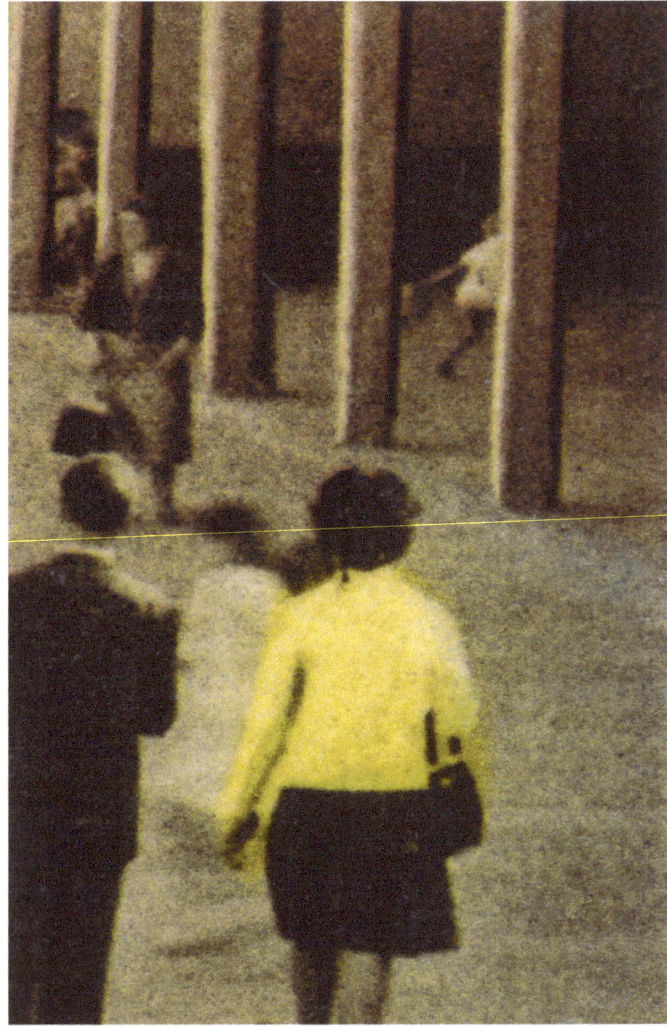

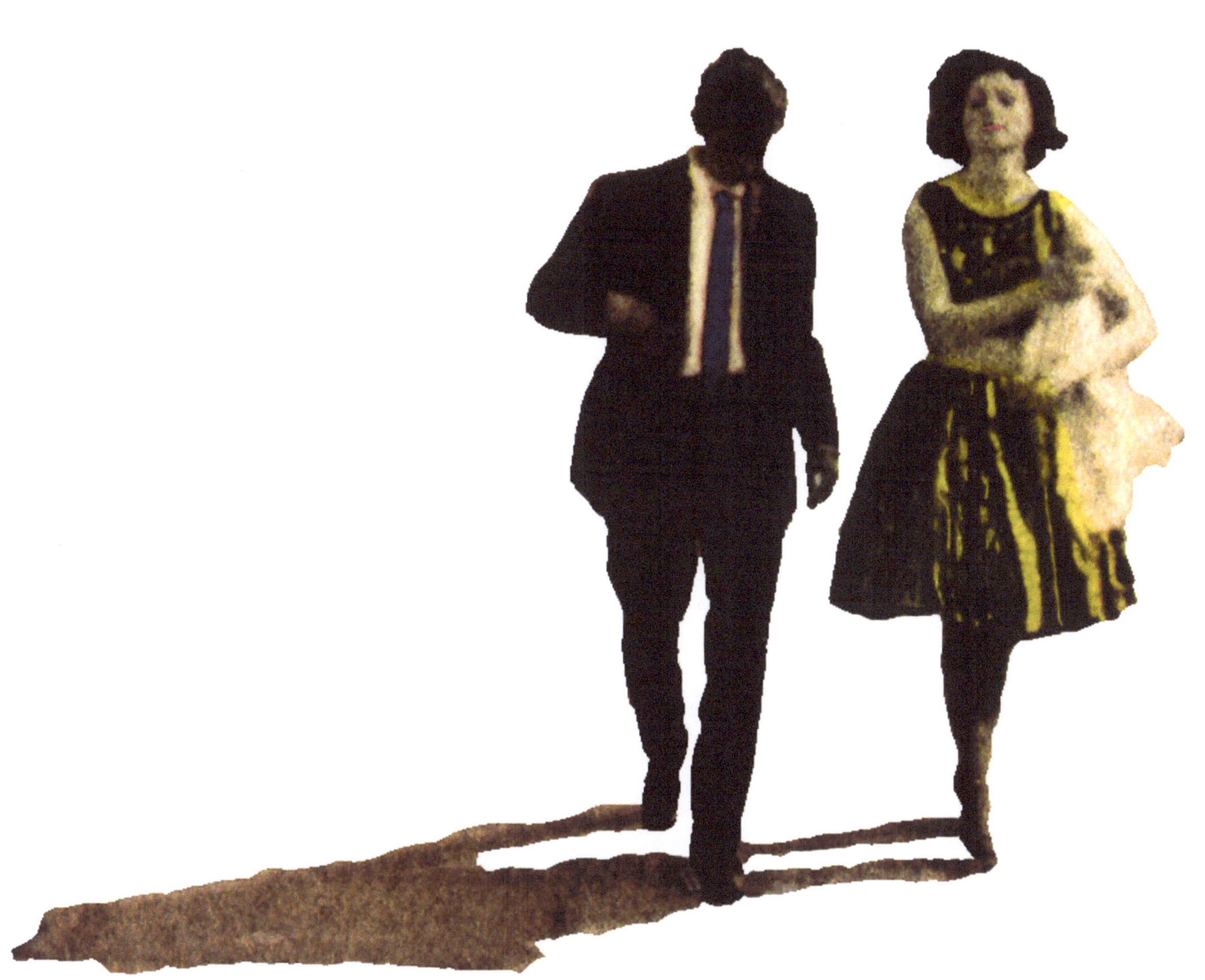